FRENCH
Twist

JANINE WINTERS

Copyright © 2024 by Janine Winters

All rights reserved. This book or any portion thereof may not be reproduced or used in any manner whatsoever without the express written permission of the publisher except for the use of brief quotations in a book review.

Publishing Services provided by Paper Raven Books LLC
Printed in the United States of America
First Printing, 2024

Cover design by Klassic Designs from 99Designs

Paperback ISBN: 979-8-9905709-0-0
Hardback ISBN: 979-8-9905709-1-7

CONTENTS

PART ONE: MOROCCO

1: In the Beginning...................................1

2: Born During War..................................3

3: Family Roots.......................................7

4: Culture and Traditions 11

5: Early Family Life.................................15

6: The Farm 27

PART TWO: ALGERIA

7: Leaving Morocco for New Possibilities...........37

8: Striving for Independence.......................41

9: Meeting Bruno...................................47

10: Visiting Dad in Prison 51

11: About Love 55

12: With Child......................................59

13: Blida 61

14: My Son is Born 63

15: Fighting All Around 65

PART THREE: FRANCE

16: Marseille and Toulon........................71

17: On the Move Again 77

18: Quincy-sous-Sénart and Cannes 79

PART FOUR: CANADA

19: O Canada!.....................................85

20: Arrival in Montreal..........................87

21: Excitement and Stress 93

22: A New Friend.................................97

23: Big Changes 103

24: Expo 67 107

25: Into the Wilderness......................... 111

26: To British Columbia......................... 119

27: Arrival on the West Coast.................... 123

28: Back to Quebec 129

29: Visit to Paris.............................. 133

30: Return to Montreal......................... 137

31: The Accident.............................. 139

32: Joy Owning a Restaurant 143

33: South for the Winter........................ 145

34: The Quiet Revolution....................... 147

35: A New Direction 151

PART FIVE: UNITED STATES

36: Living in the United States 157

37: The Florida Keys 161

38: On the Ocean 165

39: Another Chance Encounter 175

40: Ranching Florida-Style 183

41: A Jekyll and Hyde Affair 193

42: Café de France 205

43: A Visit from Immigration 211

44: Soulmates 215

45: Our Sanibel Island Vacation 219

46: Meeting John's Family 223

47: The Wedding at Café de France 227

48: Moving to Arkansas 233

49: Bad News 239

50: The Voice 243

51: Preparing to Say Goodbye 249

52: After John and Life on the Farm 251

53: Life Lessons Learned 253

Acknowledgements 255

To all those who pick up this book,
thank you for giving my words a chance.

INTRODUCTION

My name is Janine Winters, and I've lived a good life, a long one full of adventures. There are the French and Spanish bloodlines of my ancestors coursing through my veins. But there's something else, too: the spirit of a loving God who is in all things. I know that spirit has guided me, and that gives me great pleasure when I think of everything I've experienced. Some of it has been hard, some of it sad. But joy is there, as well. More than one friend has told me I should write a book. I suppose that's a bit of a cliché, but here we are, and here is my story.

PART ONE
Morocco

1

In the Beginning

Sunlight sparkled and danced across the tops of ocean waves, creating rainbows in the mist. The scent of salt was so strong I could taste it. A few sailing ships dotted the horizon. The warmth felt good on my teenage body. I was grateful to be away from family disturbances, free and independent in my youth.

Morocco has a rich history, a fascinating culture, and an atmosphere of magic. When I think of that time on the beach, it brings back many memories. This was the land of my birth, of my youth. Its influence will never be lost, though it's been decades since I left. I get nostalgic reflecting on that time.

True, it wasn't all light. There was plenty of darkness, both in the country and my own past. However, the birds, the flowers, the sun, and the sea—all were soothing and had a calming effect. I can't underestimate the importance of that.

Moroccan people at the beach wear their native clothing. It's loose and colorful. So much of this North African coastal country is like that—loose, colorful, and spicy. Spicy like the food, alive and vibrant. Yet there's also the conservative side, the one that keeps men in charge and women and children quiet. Seen but not heard.

A clear division exists between men and women. It goes back a long time. Expectations are in place. Women cook, clean, and take care of the children. Men have the freedom. They can go anywhere and pretty much do anything, even if it means abusing family members. It's not publicized, but it's too often tolerated. Yes, family is important. But traditions run deep, and in a patriarchal society, women and children don't have the same rights as men.

Sometimes we don't appreciate what we have, the basic necessities of life, or, more importantly, our resolve to live, to survive, to meet the challenges that come along.

I think about that now. I thought about it at the time, too. Back there in Morocco, land of my birth, I was a young girl, but not so young that I was unaware that something wasn't quite right in my family. My mother loved my sister, brother, and me dearly. My father was a charmer, but he had a dark side.

I later found out just how dark—a murderer!

2

Born During War

On February 3, 1943, the world was still at war. Mind-boggling when you consider the conflict had been raging for almost four years. The Second World War wasn't even supposed to happen, according to those who claimed the First World War was the "war to end all wars."

That February morning was my entry into the world. Mother awoke after midnight. Her water had broken, and labor was underway. Not a good time. Rabat, Morocco, was in a blackout. Just the day before, the Americans had warned of an impending bombing. They'd bombed us, too, but with paper flyers calling for a covering of windows at night and the turning off of all lights. Lights out meant *blackout!*

My mother was young and already had one child. My older sister, France, had been born just nineteen months earlier. Can you picture the scene? Awakened in the middle of the night, labor pains, the threat of bombs falling from the sky, a toddler in tow, and a husband away engaged in military service.

Not a good time. But what was a woman to do? Ready or not, here I come!

Making her way in the dark to her sister's house in Aguedal, my mother awakened Aunt Rosalie and Uncle Horace Garcia. They were willing to help her on this dangerous night. Thank God for them; they were our saviors. My sweet uncle agreed to take Mom to a maternity ward beyond the city. The brilliant stars in the Moroccan sky were a welcome guiding light toward the walls built to keep residents safe and intruders out. With not a little trepidation, they made it through the gates on a bicycle.

I was born in the early-morning hours on a Wednesday under the sign of Aquarius. Franklin D. Roosevelt was president of the United States, and Winston Churchill was the British prime minister. Pope Pius XII led the Catholic Church. Adolf Hitler and the Nazis were hell-bent on dominating Europe and beyond. It was a dark time, but as the saying went, "The darkest hour is right before dawn."

The Maternité Maréchal Lyautey where Mother gave birth to me was like a clinic and the closest thing to a hospital maternity ward for many in Rabat. My sister was also born there on July 14, 1941. That was the French Armistice Day, so my parents named her France Huguette. Three years after my birth, my brother came into the world at the same maternity clinic.

My sister always had a small frame, but she was the strongest and fittest kid around. She could climb the *mât de cocagne*, a very tall pole at the beach where boys and men competed. It was quite a skill to reach the top. The pole was greased, but France could scale it as if she were a monkey. Making it to the top earned her all the gifts at the end of the pole. There were many prizes, such as wine, salami, and candies, all hanging from a large ring at the top of the pole. She beat out all the others—quite the feat considering she was only twelve years old!

France was a fighter and loved to play marbles with the boys. She took her role as the eldest very seriously and had no problem being in charge of us. When Dad was around, however, it was a different story. She became scared, feared him, and was very quiet.

Alain Georges was our baby brother. He came into this world on June 16, 1946, with the cutest smile, and was a quiet little boy with curly blond hair. I was his older sister by three years, but he was my little buddy for life. For both France and me, he was our baby, but for Mom he was her little man.

The three of us had our differences, but in the end we were thick as thieves. I was the middle child and was a bigger baby at birth. It didn't take long for me to catch up with my sister's petite figure.

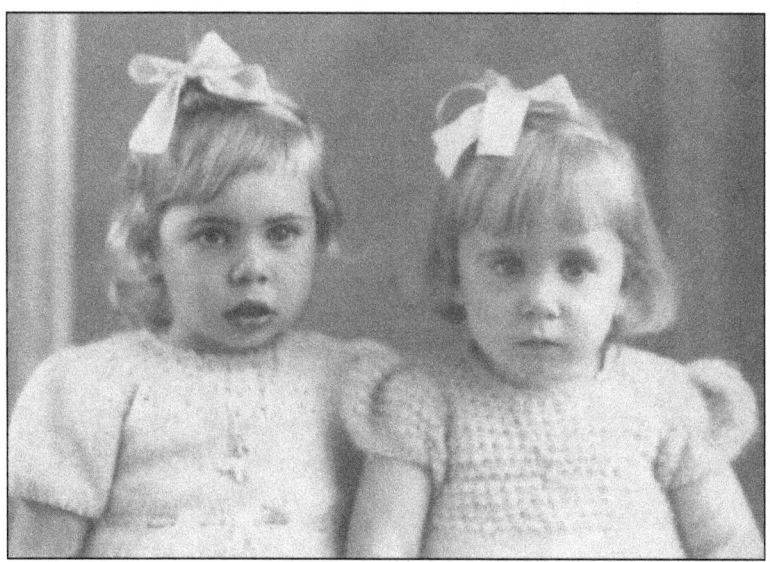

Mom dressed France and me the same, so we looked like twins. Although my sister was *délicate*, she was stronger than I was and precocious. Mom told me she spoke fluently before she was a year old!

On the other hand, I had a speech problem and one real interest: Mother's milk bags or breasts. I was Mama's girl for three years until Alain kicked me out!

I used to ask Mom where I came from, and she told me about the Maréchal Lyautey run by an army of sisters, the Catholic nuns. Each door had a picture of a flower.

"France was a rose and you a carnation!" she told me. The carnation became my flower for life.

Although France and I were close, we had real differences. She always competed with me. It seemed to me as if she had no heart and couldn't be trusted. I suppose some of that was sibling rivalry, but it went deeper than that.

Alain is very much like our father. He is so smart and has a very knowledgeable brain. He's also such an old soul! The difference between him and our dad is that he's honest and generous. For many years, he dealt in antiques in Paris and is a real character.

3

Family Roots

I'm of French and Spanish/Basque ancestry. Around 1930, my maternal grandparents left Andalusia in Spain and settled in Morocco. Food was very scarce, and famines made my grandparents quite desperate to survive. I remember hearing tales of eating out of garbage bins. Hunger will do that to you.

With five children, they were quite poor. My mother, Candide Moguel, was just three years old at the time. The family walked to the Strait of Gibraltar and crossed into Morocco. From there, they traveled by mule and carriage along the coast.

They were more than willing to work for food. Dealing with harsh conditions left a deep impression on my mother. I saw her tears when she recalled a special moment with her mother, sharing a bag of fresh figs, the children all crying from hunger pangs.

People often lived short lives in those days. I have no memories of my mother's parents, since they had both died when I was quite young. On the other hand, I do remember my paternal grandmother. Those memories aren't fond ones.

Esperanza Pupo was from Cadiz, Spain. She smelled funny, had hair on her chin, and never took a liking to me. She ignored me during most of her visits, but as I grew older, I heard her mention that I didn't look like Dad. And I could feel her anger. Esperanza suspected her son wasn't my biological father and didn't hide the suspicion.

She doted on France, who was her favorite, and my sister often talked Grandma into giving her sweets. France then gave some to Alain and me.

I tried to stay away from my grandmother; it was difficult to be nice to her. My sister resembled my dad, but I looked like Mom. Grandma accused my mother of having an affair, and therefore she believed I was a bastard child!

Sunday was visiting day. Aunt Ana was a teenager then, and she was our babysitter. We loved her because she read us books and told stories, sometimes scary ones. I remember her singing once about a mother who remarried to a very bad man and died, leaving the children to him. I'll never forget that day!

Aunt Ana often took the three of us to Grandma's shack. We started early on Sunday morning. Mom prepared our bath with a big pot of water in the fire pit. She checked our heads for lice and rubbed our bodies with soap, finishing with a rinse of vinegar.

Grandma had a huge garden in her backyard with peach trees, chickens, and ducks. She never invited me inside her house. As I said, she didn't care for me, so I sat in a rocking chair on the porch and was grateful when our visits were short.

4

Culture and Traditions

North Africa and the scenic countries of Morocco and Algeria have always attracted visitors, peaceful and otherwise. It is beautiful with a rugged coastline and full of rich Mediterranean history. Barbary pirates, slave traders, and foreign conquerors from various ancient empires—Greeks, Phoenicians, Romans, and later Arabs during the Muslim conquest—all came ashore.

When I was a child, Morocco was still somewhat primitive. It wasn't unusual to see goats, camels, donkeys, snakes, and scorpions. Despite our more primitive society, the French government took care to provide food, security, and education. There were immunizations and some medical care. Allocations were made to help children and build schools. This was fortunate for the many who didn't have the means to provide some of the basic needs of life.

If you were educated, your stature was elevated. However, adult literacy wasn't prevalent in our country. To read and write wasn't merely a privilege; it was a badge of honor because it was uncommon. I'm grateful we were educated because if you were able to go to school, that was a plus. Just getting the children fed was often difficult, so school wasn't the first priority. That's what happens when you live in poverty.

French was the official language in Morocco. School was taught in French, with Arabic as a second language. But there were also many people who spoke Spanish, since for a time Spain was involved in the country's rule.

After the Second World War, the United States built military bases in Morocco, and the locals all had to learn English if they wanted jobs there. The postwar years brought changes. There's a lot of diversity in Morocco, and much of that's due to its history of various inhabitants who each brought their own way of life. The mix of cultures and traditions has resulted in a rich blend of food, music, art, and religion.

In my youth, I enjoyed the land, culture, and food of Morocco. But it's hard to describe the anxiety of living in such a volatile country. There was a lot of unrest. Moroccans wanted their freedom. They're a proud people with a deep history. To continue under the rule of a combined protectorate of France and Spain was restrictive. Over the course of my first ten years of life, there was often a feeling that a revolution might break out at any time. Combining that with the challenging circumstances at home presented a lot to bear for a young girl.

The French Protectorate began in 1912. The sultan at that time was Abd al-Hafid, and after many months of negotiation, he signed the Treaty of Fez. The French sent him into exile to a palace in Tangier. His brother, Yusef, was then proclaimed sultan by the French administration.

There was a change in 1927 with the sudden death of Yusef. His son, Mohammed V, succeeded him as the new sultan. He continued as the

Moroccan king during the years leading up to the Second World War, through the war, and in the years afterward. In 1940, the French-German Armistice resulted in anti-Jewish sentiment across southern France where they were now under the rule of a new collaborationist government based in Vichy. Mohammed V opposed Vichy's anti-Jewish legislation, which made him unpopular with the French.

In 1947, the sultan demanded independence for Morocco in his famous Tangier Speech. He had his son and future king of Morocco, Hassan II, by his side, and his speech sparked violent reactions and riots across the nation. Needless to say, that made the French furious. In 1953, they arrested Mohammed V and sent him and his family into exile on Corsica. Later, they were all transferred to Madagascar, but in 1955 they returned.

November 18, 1955 was a sunny day, but more than sunlight warmed the hearts of Moroccans. Mohammed V made a majestic return to his beloved country, parading through the streets and receiving an extremely warm welcome from the people who had dearly missed him during his exile.

Mohammed V negotiated Morocco's freedom from both the French and Spanish, and independence was finally officially declared on March 2, 1956. A year later, Mohammed began his reign as the king of a liberated Morocco.

5

Early Family Life

My parents met at a youth camp in Rabat. My dad was twenty-two, my mother seventeen. They were so young, practically still kids. In 1939 in Africa, a young woman had to stay "clean" until marriage. No fooling around! So they got married with my grandfather's blessing and moved into the Quartier de l'Océan in a *mauresque* house with an interior tile courtyard and a fountain in the center. It was quite lovely.

There were other families with children living in adjacent houses connected to our courtyard. We were all close in age, and it was like one big extended family. We walked to school together and had the same teachers.

The ocean was two small streets away from our home. I can still recall the sound of crashing waves and the scent of the sea. The Atlantic Ocean provided plenty of fish and shellfish. The tang was ever-present; the *crachin*, or drizzle, kept a rhythmic beat along with a cool spray.

At low tide, we headed out at night, carrying lanterns to light our way. When the ocean retreated from the shore, we grabbed crabs and squids in the shallow pools the waves had left behind. It was a place of exploration and adventure. I could play and splash in these pools. But there was also the reward of the seafood we captured and brought home.

The food in Morocco was fresh and delicious. Street vendors grilled lamb and goat and put the meat on sticks, coated with the hot and tasty harissa that was part of so much Moroccan cuisine.

Full of Spanish- and French-speaking Catholics, the quartier de l'Océan was akin to living in a small town. We were refugees, or from refugee parents, and we stayed close as a group of Spanish speakers.

Life at home was difficult. My father could be cruel and unpredictable. When he had a good day, it was good for all of us. In public, he was charming and sociable, very organized and well informed. Dad was a handsome man and always quite fit. He loved soccer and was part of a group that often met to practice. But his biggest interests were the ocean and underwater diving. He was an excellent swimmer even in rough waters.

My father's love of the sea led him to work along the beaches with the Control Civil in Rabat, helping to spot and rescue swimmers or others who were in danger of drowning. Willis ambulance trucks patrolled the seashore. Although not physically big, my father was muscular and well suited for the job.

He loved underwater swimming and was fascinated by the French oceanographer and naval officer Jacques Cousteau. As a result, he was one of the first to acquire and use an underwater breathing apparatus, the so-called Aqua-Lung developed by Cousteau and Émile Gagnan, an Air Liquide engineer.

Father snorkeled and taught us to do so. France, my sister, refused to snorkel with him, but Alain and I were happy to join him. He taught us about underwater "snakes," the dangerous moray eel, or *murène*, and not to touch them.

One time, we were out in a boat, and Dad asked Alain and me to jump into the ocean. Our seafaring vessel was just a small fishing boat. It was scary, but I knew I had to do it! I confronted my fear and didn't want Dad to get mad or mock us as he would with my sister. We couldn't tell him no. We had to do it. I'm sure it impressed him when we did.

When he was in a good mood, Dad could be the best. He could be fun and happy at times. Too bad those occasions weren't more frequent.

My father was probably the most intelligent person I'd ever met. He had a good business mind and loved sports, so it wasn't uncommon to find him among a group of men playing soccer.

Fortune smiled on him, but I can't say he earned it honestly. There was mystery surrounding his dealings. Later, we came to know that he was a criminal. I can't say for certain whether or not his criminal inclination was hereditary. But it might have been when considering his family roots.

The history on my father's side included generations of wheelers and dealers that can be traced right back to Spain and Italy and the area around the Mediterranean Sea. In about 1900, some of them settled in North Africa.

My father was an only child and his father, my paternal grandfather, José Navarro, was of Spanish and Basque heritage. Born in Oran, Algeria, on December 16, 1890, he died at an early age. He was only thirty-three years old when he passed away from typhus in Marrakech, Morocco, leaving a widow bride—my grandmother—and his only son, my father, now fatherless at the tender age of three.

Jean Navarro, my father, was born on March 7, 1921. He grew up in Morocco, living by the sea and learning from his father, who undoubtedly learned from his father, and so on down the line. What they learned and the kind of things they did were in the name of making a living. But I know that my father also pursued a life that rewarded him for illegal activities. A crafty man, he used politics to help cover his crimes.

Some will say the sins of the father are passed on to his heirs. True or not, it sure felt as if we were suffering unfairly. Life wasn't easy with Dad. My relationship with him was often a rocky one. Mother and my siblings knew this, as well, and had to put up with our father's bad temper.

Although Father was hard on us, in public he could be quite charming and sociable. A very organized man and well informed, he employed his charm to manipulate others. If he didn't get his way, though, look out! And woe to us if he came home angry or upset. I endured his violent character in those first ten years of my life. Later, it became an ongoing cycle of violence.

In Morocco, it's common practice for all businesses and schools to close daily at noon for two hours, a rule picked up from the French, who believe sitting for a proper lunch is the way to have the most important meal of the day.

When we had lunch with our parents, Dad used this quiet mealtime to ask us about our lessons. He sat at the head of the table, and we knew then that the interrogation would soon start.

We hoped he'd be in a good mood. He was very severe, and if we forgot the answers, he got frustrated.

"Come now, you must know the answer. Think!" he demanded. "I'm sure my children are smarter than you're showing with this pitiful display."

Every time he quizzed France, she stared at him, and many times simply started to cry.

Although I had a "thick" tongue, I was a quick thinker. I often surprised Dad with answers to help my sister. He tested me with very long and difficult words, but I was able to give him the right answers, which made him proud and nicer toward me.

"Well done, my bright young daughter!" he praised. "France, you could learn a thing or two from your younger smart sister."

Later, I realized that created jealousy with my siblings.

Those were horrible moments that broke my heart. I wondered if he enjoyed playing us off against one another. We were afraid to upset our dad and loved when he was away at work or employed out of town.

I'm quite sure Mother suffered from our father's temperament. He didn't show appreciation and could be cruel, but that didn't deter her from finding ways to put her gift of compassion and kindness to good use. She took a job at a military hospital where she trained to care for terminally ill soldiers. Mom loved this new job. It was conveniently just five minutes from our home. She was happy at work, and the good benefits helped our family. The job also gave her time away from Father's meanness.

My early life was very much oriented toward my mother's family. They were from Spain, and my maternal grandfather chose to return in 1945, not wanting to die away from his beloved homeland. The family went with him, but he soon passed away, and my grandmother came back to Rabat where she lived out the rest of her days.

Much of the family came once a year to visit, bringing Spain with them. They loved to sing and dance flamenco. The Spanish city of Seville would have been proud.

Aunt Rosalie and her husband, Horace, were the centers of our extended family. My father never cared much for them. They were a large, proud, and close-knit family from Seville. There were five sisters, Esperanza, Rosalie,

Antoinette, Candide, and Eliane, along with three brothers, Manolo, Louis, and the youngest, Horacito. My father called my mother's family *le clan des Moguel*. Their home was always open to us, and we gathered for holidays or birthdays—uncles, aunts, and cousins.

The wood chalet had big, covered porches with tables and chairs and climbing grapes. I've never tasted better grapes in my life and can still close my eyes today and smell and taste the golden goodness.

It seemed there were always many people around. The men prepared the *méchoui*, lamb roast, cooking it outside in a big fire on a spit. The ladies in the kitchen prepared *tajine*, a hearty stew with vegetables, and couscous. I loved to help harvest, cut, and wash the vegetables. Most days we served thirty or forty people, and that's how I learned to help in a kitchen.

My mother and Aunt Rosalie were in charge, and I enjoyed being their helper. "Here, Janine, chop these vegetables," Mom told me, "but be careful not to cut yourself." I did as she asked. "Good job!"

I ate up the compliments, which nourished my self-esteem as much as the tasty food my mother and aunt prepared.

Mom's sisters and brothers were all married and had several children. Most Sundays were spent at Rosalie's with cousins and friends. If it was a holiday, such as Christmas, we celebrated all the more.

Morocco is a Muslim country, but that didn't deter these Spaniards. While we typically ate the local cuisine, on these special festive occasions, we also feasted on turkey and homemade stuffing with couscous.

The "clan" didn't trust my dad, and I sometimes overheard disparaging remarks about him. As time went on, I discovered more of his bad nature. I was ten when my parents had a big fight, and Dad hurt Mom.

"How dare you question my ways!" he once screamed at Mother. "And your family, always so smug and suspicious. Never forget that I'm the provider. I put food on the table."

Then there was a slap and a cry. It caused me great emotional pain to know he was hurting Mom. Yet it continued. He became more and more violent.

One day, he packed his bags and left for Spain, running from something illegal he was involved with. It happened so suddenly. He was gone just like that!

Around the same time, a riot broke out in Casablanca concerning Tunisian union leaders. One of them, Fehrat Hashed, was murdered. 3,000 protestors attempted to storm the Casablanca police station, and in the ensuing violence, at least twenty-five Moroccans were killed. Troops were brought in to restore order, which produced a lot of bad blood and anti-French sentiment. Depending on one's view of history, this was either an unruly mob engaged in reactive violence or the growing defiance against French colonialism by nationalist Moroccans. Many longed for independence, and the early 1950s was a time of great unrest.

With Dad away, Mother reacted immediately. Her move to protect us was to enroll us in Tiflet Boarding School, an hour away from Rabat, which was quite a change for us. Up to that time, my siblings and I attended the local école des Jardins in Rabat. We walked there, just a mile across fields of wheat or wild red poppies. Most days we ate at the school cafeteria where we were served home-cooked soups, French bread, and milk. The only dessert was fruit, but it was delicious and nourishing.

The weather in Morocco is perfect for growing fruits and vegetables. Morocco might not be a rich country according to monetary wealth, but the soil is fertile and the temperature moderate, almost tropical, typically between sixty-three and eighty-four degrees Fahrenheit. Our friends and family planted groves of oranges, grapefruit, and lemons. It was also a productive environment for bananas.

Grapes, too, prosper in the soil and temperatures of Morocco. Many of the grapes in the vineyards yield a high degree of alcohol. The French in Morocco knew about wine, but since Muslims didn't drink alcohol, most of it was shipped to France.

In the winemaking process, the grapes' sugars are converted into alcohol, so the more time they have to mature, the boozier the end product. The climate is a big factor where grapes are grown. Cooler temperatures in places such as Germany result in less-sweet styles of wine, while warm regions such as Argentina, Australia, and California make for rich, full-bodied varieties.

At the time, as I've said, Morocco was ruled by the French Protectorate, but life was easier thanks to the nearby American bases, which provided jobs, my first taste of Coca-Cola, and my first sight of black-and-white television. They also certainly helped to furnish education for children. Learning English was very popular, and the radio from US bases was the only music after years of war and destruction.

Once I understood the history of the European rule of Morocco, it made me better appreciate the influences of both Spain and France, as well as the deep pride Moroccans have for their land and culture. As I noted before, there was a lot of tension in the years after the First World War, which took place as a backdrop to my early years and the tensions in our family. They were two parallel worlds: the fight for Moroccan independence and the struggle of our family for freedom from my dad. Sometimes the best escape for me was to be at school away from family drama and surrounded by others my age.

One day, the teacher announced that we had a new student. Her name was Carol, which reminded me of Neil Sedaka's "Oh! Carol." We used to sing that song together. Such fun!

It didn't take long for her to learn French, and from her I picked up my first taste of English. She taught me "Twinkle, Twinkle, Little Star," a simple children's song.

Most of the time we didn't understand each other, but we still became friends and were inseparable. Just a smile or a giggle could convey enough meaning. We just clicked.

Carol's dad was a soldier on a US base in Kenitra, but he was transferred after one year. I thought often of Carol and know she planted a seed—the dream of going to America! It was far, far away out west in the same direction as our awesome sunsets.

"Carol," I told her, "someday I'll live in America. I'll live a life I've always dreamed about!"

When she smiled slyly, it seemed to me she was implying she knew something about the United States that I didn't. And, of course, she did! But I didn't know that until many years later when I had my own experiences in the country. We sat for hours watching the sun until it "disappeared" into the ocean, my mind filled with thoughts of the bright, shiny faraway land of freedom.

The seed that Carol planted did indeed lead to a destination and a dream. Now, many years later, I'm so proud to grow old in America and am the perfect example that dreams can come true.

Those dreams were at times obscured by the nightmare of my father's dark life. It surely took a toll on our mother, but her main concern was for our welfare. Mom rode the bus every Sunday so she could take us away from the school grounds to a terrace to drink Coca-Cola and eat delicious pastries. She never complained when we waited impatiently for her.

My mother was a kind and loving parent, but when necessary, she protected us like a lioness watching over her cubs. When my father returned from Spain, we were still attending the boarding school. He agreed to the arrangement on one condition: Mom had to move back in with him. He was involved in the real-estate business and was using her to cover some of his shady dealings.

Later, my parents agreed to a divorce, but it was a scam on Dad's part to hide his income. He put his properties in her name and got away with it. In Morocco, the man is the boss of his wife and children. She wasn't able to handle the business without a male involved, yet Dad had contrived ways to keep himself out of trouble using our mother as part of his schemes. Mom agreed to all this on one condition: she was to retain custody of the children in the divorce.

One night, my father told the three of us about the divorce. "Children," he began, "your mother and I aren't going to stay married. But it's not that we're really breaking up. It's a way to help maintain some business interests. You have to trust me about this. Believe me, it's for the best."

There it was. He informed us that it wasn't real and was only to protect his real-estate assets. For me, it was a release, since I wished we could walk away from him.

Dad was mean to Mom and often called her names. Sometimes she defended herself, even though that put her in greater danger. She knew too much about his dealings, and we often heard them arguing. It wasn't clear what they were talking about, but the sound of their voices was enough for us to be afraid that something awful was going to happen. We could hear Mom accusing him and warning him to stop. Our father had bought our first refrigerator, and in one of his acts of madness, he took an ax to it. It was a violent display and gave us a terrible feeling. When he realized what he'd done, he replaced the refrigerator.

One of the things that bothered him a lot was how I was growing up. My body was quickly changing, and I looked older than my age.

"Janine," Dad would say, "you're growing into a young woman. I suppose you must have started your monthly time. Your breasts are certainly developing. You need to know more about these things. We can talk."

"No!" was my initial reaction. "Dad, I understand you're trying to be helpful, but to be honest, you're making me very uncomfortable when you say things like that. I just don't want to talk about sex!"

I wanted to spend more time with my friends, which Dad was against. I came home from school one day but had gone to the theater first. He was so upset that he grabbed me. "You're lying! Why do you lie to me? You've been out with boys, haven't you?"

He didn't believe my explanation and accused me of lying. The next thing he did was to pick up a big pair of scissors and cut my bangs! That outraged me. Even though I was terrified and somewhat numb, I pushed him. "How dare you!" I cried out. "Look at what you've done." I guess something in me just snapped. As you might imagine, that only made things worse.

Despite being humiliated and saddened, I wasn't afraid of him. I stood my ground. Sometimes I think he admired my spirit, though it made him furious. Thankfully, the boarding school gave me time away. It was such a blessing to have a break from these family crises. For sure, I missed Mother. I was lonely and looked forward to her visits.

6

The Farm

Dad bought an old farm in 1955. There were orchards of grapefruit, oranges, and lemons. He decided we should move there. This was out in the country, which made it difficult to get around. I had to take a bus that dropped me off at a stop, but with a good thirty-minute walk from there to the farm. If I didn't make good time, I faced suspicions from my father. He always wanted to know our schedule and even started spying on us.

I knew some of his distrust was because my body was changing, making me look more like a woman. He could be overly protective. Worse, he began to eye me in a way that made both my mother and me uncomfortable.

I didn't want to be alone with him. He kept interrogating me about sex every time, which was very disturbing.

"Janine, you're becoming such a beautiful woman. Men will soon want to know you better, to be with you. You understand that, don't you? They'll want to have you, to have your body, if that hasn't already happened."

Sex was taboo! No one ever talked about it in front of me. There was no sex education at school, no textbook, nothing. Everything I knew came from my friends at school.

As a normal teenager, I was brought up to be respectful. However, I didn't trust my dad. He complained about my clothes, especially my bathing suit. I was a teenager and ready to be me, to be free of his harsh and controlling ways.

The school uniform was an off-white blouse down to my knees. I didn't care for this long blouse over my clothes required by the Collège des Orangers. I wanted to shorten the sleeves to make it my style, but Dad got very upset.

"What do you think you're doing with your uniform?" he demanded. "It's fine the way it is. You know I paid to have it altered."

"You had it altered?"

"That's right! Your mom had it made by a seamstress, but I thought it was too different from the usual uniform, so I asked her to make it more traditional."

I tried to explain why I wanted to change the uniform. "I want a style that makes me feel confident and unique."

"Well, you're just inviting trouble. It's important to follow the school dress code and maintain a sense of uniformity among the students. But if you're so intent on changing it, then I'll take care of it."

He took scissors to the blouse and cut it all up, which both angered and frightened me.

"You've ruined it," I screamed. "Look at what you've done!" Tears streamed down my face. Dad merely shrugged and walked away, making me feel more frustrated and scared.

When it came to the way I dressed or appeared, I was becoming more aware that something was wrong. Why did he care so much? Was he really just being overly protective? I began to sense it was something else.

Children never want to think their parents might treat them poorly. Some kids aren't cared for properly. Worse, others are abused. My father saw me becoming a woman, but what he might be really thinking truly bothered me.

I became so frightened of being alone with him that I got sick. I wanted to die, so I stopped eating and drinking. I rubbed the thermometer so it showed a higher temperature, hoping Mother would believe I had a fever. She was clearly worried. During that time, she had me admitted to Hôpital Marie Feuillet. I missed a lot of school, a whole semester. Eventually, I returned to boarding school.

My father often played roulette and got richer. Additionally, he dealt in real estate and used me to write numerous letters about his businesses. He coached me on how to do this by employing different letterheads and names. I think he was training me to be a criminal like him! To be honest, I liked helping him and enjoyed being part of his projects, even though I realized I was writing fake letters.

The more someone gets involved in illegal matters, the harder it is to keep them quiet. Actions have a tendency to catch up with us. One night, Dad came home and told Mom he'd stolen some equipment from work. The police were onto him, were asking questions, and becoming increasingly suspicious. But he hid the equipment in the basement, and no one came to question him further. He got away with it! I wished he hadn't, though I never saw him so scared and anxious.

France was attending a Catholic school at the time. All her teachers were nuns. She mentioned the situation at home, and they offered to take her in, allowing her to live at the school with them, even though the place wasn't officially a boarding institution. The nuns were concerned and willing to protect her, but France chose not to take them up on their proposal.

Meanwhile, I was constantly defending myself. I knew Dad was spying on me. I began to worry that he was going to kill me! Maybe that was irrational, but again, as a young girl witnessing his mean temper, it was easy to imagine such things. Dad couldn't stand my disobedience, and there were times when he took his fury out by hurting Mom or my sweet brother. They were growing more concerned, too.

One time, Alain went hunting. He had a BB gun and had fun in the forest by himself. It was close to the farm, but he must have lost track of time. He was supposed to meet Dad at the barbershop, but he was late. When Alain finally made it home, Dad beat him. My father kicked him so hard in the leg that a bone broke. Mom took Alain to the hospital where she worked, and a cast was put on his leg. It was painful for Alain—and for us to witness it. Of course, Mom was embarrassed and worried. She kept telling us the divorce would be final and our life would change for the better.

On another occasion, my father met me at the bus stop. He was waiting for me, and it was clear he was unhappy. I got into the car, and he slapped me. "I saw you playing in the schoolyard with boys!" he yelled.

That accusation stung, as if he'd slapped me again. I didn't know what he was talking about. But I couldn't get him to listen to me.

"Stop!" I cried. "I... I wasn't. What do you mean? I was coming home, Dad."

He just kept hitting me. When we got home, I jumped out of the car and ran.

It was getting dark, but I just wanted to get away. My fear grew by the moment, worrying that he'd hurt me some more. I managed to climb up the side of the house near the well. Misjudging a jump, I slipped and very nearly fell. The shaft below was at least 100 feet deep. The fall probably would have killed me, but somehow I regained my balance and continued climbing up to the roof.

Lying flat on the roof gave me a good view of things. Dad was yelling at Mom.

"Where is she?" he demanded. "That girl is up to no good. I'll teach her a lesson."

He was searching for me, shining a flashlight and casting eerie shadows through the fruit trees. I held my breath. As soon as I was able to, I waved at Mom. She realized it was me and got really mad at my father. We left the house that night and made it to Aunt Rosalie's. A few days later, Dad apologized and we returned home. He left me alone, but only for a while.

Alain was still recovering from his broken leg. All around it was an unhappy situation. Mom again assured us the divorce would soon be final and our life would change for the better. We started plotting our escape. I think we all realized that staying was hopeless. No one wanted to be trapped with a madman.

Then a day came when Dad confronted me about some pictures. I'd had passport photos taken and had given a few to my friends at school.

"Janine, you had some new passport pictures taken. Where are they?"

I lied. "I must have lost them."

But he fooled me. "I know you gave them away. To boys, right?"

He opened his hand to show me six pictures. I didn't realize they were the ones he'd tricked me into reordering earlier. I really believed he'd somehow gotten hold of the ones I'd given to my friends. So I admitted I'd lied.

"You little liar!" he exploded. "Just like your mother." He then called me names the same way he did with Mom when he was mad at her.

Dad had sent Alain to town to buy bullets for his gun. I knew he'd done this so he could be alone with me. I went to my room, sat on the bed, opened a newspaper, and acted as if I was interested in the articles. Dad stormed into the room like a tiger and slapped my face.

"You think you can lie to my face and get away with it!" he shouted.

I tried to defend myself, kicking as hard as I could with my feet. He struck me again, and my nose began to bleed. Then he pushed my face down on the open newspaper, and I rolled to the floor, where he kicked me against the side of the bed. I must have passed out. I remember waking up to the sound of water running. Realizing he was in the other bathroom, I escaped by jumping out a window.

Banged up and bloody, I ran across fields and groves. Finally, I came to someone's home, stumbled into the courtyard, and sought refuge. A young man came out, and I begged him to let me use his telephone. "Please, you must help me!"

He appeared concerned, of course, because of my beat-up condition. Thankfully, he agreed to let me use his phone.

I called Mom and told her what had happened. "Mamita, something has to be done. Dad hit me, and I'm afraid he'll hurt me again."

Things were so out of control and desperate that I felt as if my own father was hunting me the way he would a wild animal. Thinking back on those times, I believe he was trying to get us out of the house by creating chaos.

Mom, Alain, and I moved into an apartment above Aunt Eliane's place. Dad was furious, but there was nothing he could do to force us back home. We tried to live a normal life, but with my father there was no normal.

I was the reason my mom left him. She was willing to do whatever was necessary to protect me. I knew that sooner or later he'd make me pay.

Each day as I bicycled to Collège des Orangers, I dreaded another encounter with him. It finally happened one afternoon as I was going home for lunch. I was pedaling down the middle of a hill when I heard the engine of his car slow down. The car stopped alongside me, and he opened the passenger door and pointed a gun at me. "If your mother doesn't come back, I'll kill you!"

I didn't want my mother to go back, and I told him so. That made it a sad day for me. I was trapped and remember wanting to die. Then I wanted to kill him. The saddest thing was I had no one to confide in, no friend with whom I could share my pain.

Eventually, my parents were legally divorced, and Mom got custody of her three children. We began making plans to leave Morocco and move to Algeria. Mom prepared our passports with the French embassy and bought our plane tickets. We moved to a hotel near the airport to spend our last night. Several family members came to say goodbye. We were so scared he'd find us, and it was only when the airplane took off that we realized we were free!

PART TWO
Algeria

Leaving Morocco for New Possibilities

It was my first time on an airplane, and I was thrilled yet anxious. Passenger flight in the 1950s was considered the golden age of flying, but it was a luxury most people couldn't afford. It could also be risky. In those days, the chances of dying in plane crashes were five times greater than today.

Somehow we managed to secure a flight out from Morocco. Before we could board the plane, we had to endure a body search. A lady escorted all of us to a room where we were told to strip.

"Put your money and valuables on a table," we were ordered. Then came a very humiliating command. "Open your legs."

Our bags were also inspected. We three kids each had a chain with the picture of Our Lady Mary, the mother of Jesus. It wasn't unusual to have jewelry of this type, since we'd all been baptized Catholics. Most Europeans fleeing from Morocco hid their valuables. Being young, I suppose it didn't occur to us to conceal ours.

As we boarded the plane, we looked around nervously and at one another. The doors to the aircraft were shut, and a flight attendant came over and handed us postcards with a picture of the airplane, a souvenir for our journey. She also gave us magazines and newspapers to pass the time with.

The flight was short but loud. We didn't say much. We had no idea where we were going but held on to the belief that anything would be better than returning to our father.

We landed in Algeria. Waiting for us at the airport was Aunt Antoinette, our mother's sister, and her husband, Antoine. They were concerned about us and had made preparations for us to be safe in our new environment. Several of our family members had already settled in Oran following the independence of Morocco. They believed Algeria would remain under French rule and that our lives would be better.

My mother was still relatively young, only thirty-six. France was sixteen, I was fifteen, and Alain was twelve. We were just children, and the bond between us was complicated and influenced by both our parents and how we were treated.

I've said it before: Mom and Dad had different personalities. But it's worth repeating to understand how much it affected us as children in the middle of their disputes. Dad was mean, conniving, and manipulative. But he was also very charismatic. Mom was nurturing and fiercely protective. She was a vibrant woman, our leader, our rock!

Mother was only three years old when her family immigrated to Morocco from her native Spain. Her life hadn't been easy, and she was tougher than any human I've ever known. I wanted to be like her. She could be so calm and gentle. Plus, she was funny. She enjoyed telling us stories and giving us pet names. Mom always put us first and protected us.

My father, on the other hand, wasn't someone I wanted to be like. I knew he was smart, but he was also dangerous. I was thrilled to get away from him. He had become a real threat to me personally as well as to the rest of the family.

We left Morocco to escape a situation that was causing a lot of anguish for us. It had become perilous to remain there, with Dad living the life of a criminal. And it was traumatic. We were all frightened that he would find us. All too soon we discovered we'd traded one threatening situation for another.

Algeria at this time was in turmoil. Many in the country were fighting for independence from France, which made descendants of French or other European countries enemies. Still, our relief escaping Dad was tangible. Oran was a vibrant port and commercial center on the Mediterranean coast and across the sea from the French Riviera. The city was filled with historical buildings, ancient mosques, and beautiful trees. There were also a multitude of private beaches, something that became important to a teenage girl searching for new experiences.

Imagine leaving the only home I'd known for what we hoped would be a new life free from the violence and dangers of war, only to realize we were back in a similar situation. Morocco had gained independence from the French. Now Algeria was fighting to do the same thing, and we were caught in the middle!

We lived on the edge, tired and isolated, with an uncertain future. But life wasn't all bad. We had relatives, such as Aunt Antoinette and her husband, Antoine, living in Oran. Our aunt and uncle were concerned for us and our safety and had made preparations for our new environment. Several of our family members had relocated to Oran after the independence of Morocco. Assurances had been given that Algeria would stay French. Later, we discovered that wasn't to be the case.

Ethnic Europeans from France and Spain who had settled in Algeria were known as *pieds-noirs*. We were considered part of this group and were disliked by Arab and Berber Algerians who no longer wanted to be under French control. Independence was bitterly opposed by the *pieds-noirs*, as well as by many members of the French military. A campaign of open rebellion by the Organisation armée secrète (OAS) led to escalating tensions and revolts. The French government and its military were declared an "occupying power."

The Évian Accords were established to guarantee the rights and safety of *pieds-noirs*, many of whom were born in Algeria. Protection was also extended to the Sephardic Jews in an independent Algeria. It was easy to see how all these different groups, some with competing agendas, were a volatile mix. Rumors spread among our people that our choice would be between "the suitcase or the coffin."

8

Striving for Independence

The French occupied Algiers in 1830 and put Algeria under their rule for a long time. After the Second World War, there was a thirst for independence from European rule and influence in North Africa. Moroccan freedom now inspired unrest and a desire for freedom in our new homeland.

Algeria was and is a predominantly Muslim country, but in the 1950s it was also home to about 1.5 million *pieds-noirs*. These ethnic French and Spanish, mostly Catholics, were often at odds with the Arabs and Berbers in the country.

The country extends from the Mediterranean coast, occupied by most of the people, to the sparsely populated Sahara, a forbidding desert where some of the hottest temperatures on the planet have been recorded. Oran, where we lived, is part of the scenic Barbary Coast and has a distinctly European ambience. The city's layout was inspired by Nice's seafront, which is called *la promenade des Anglais*. I was surprised by the diversity of people as well as by the incredible display of flowers and palm trees. It was something of a paradise, and to a young girl approaching womanhood, it was also enticing in other ways.

My family and I had been through years of frightening riots and violence during Morocco's fight for independence. The fight for freedom from French rule in Algeria caused even more fear and stress for our family. It was a civil war, but the enemy didn't wear uniforms. The Front de Libération Nationale (FLN) was comprised of Arab and Berber Algerians without a formal army and could easily be our neighbors. Meanwhile, the French-backed military had superior numbers, but the FLN was a determined group intent on becoming free of colonial rule. The conflict began in 1954 and lasted eight years. Our arrival was at a time when the war was reaching its peak. Violence in the streets was intensifying, and there we were, caught in the middle and striving to find a home and safety. It was incredibly dangerous!

In April 1962, Algeria finally achieved independence, spurring a flight of *pieds-noirs* and pro-French Algerian Arabs to Europe. By late May, hundreds of thousands had emigrated, mostly to the metropolitan areas of France. Several of our Moguel family members had moved to Oran after the independence of Morocco. They had believed Algeria would stay French, so they weren't anxious to move to Europe, at least not yet.

Uncle Antoine was a retired military man, while Aunt Antoinette was quite bossy. With the help of her husband, they planned our future, which was good, since Mom was disoriented and numb from our experience in Morocco with our father. She really needed the support of her family.

My uncle and aunt had four children of their own, all around the same age as my siblings and me. They were all sweet like their parents. We bonded with them and sought comfort in their company.

Uncle Antoine was a successful businessman and owned a mechanic shop that did a healthy business of auto repairs. He was a good man and very supportive. I loved him very much and often wished he was my real father.

In a way, they did become my family. I had a preferred cousin in Oran. Françoise was ten years older than I was and married to Roger Federici. They had two young children and had followed our aunt's move to Oran a few months earlier.

Françoise was the firstborn of the Moguel clan's five sisters. She and her husband were a reassuring presence to our family. Roger worked as a police officer, and we loved spending time with them. It made Mom happy. Françoise was like another daughter to her. We stayed with them at their apartment in Cité Perret, a twenty-two-story modern tower complete with stores and conveniences. It was something I'd never experienced. How exciting!

Aunt Antoinette found Mom a job as a maid cleaning hotel rooms. Our mother was a hard worker and appreciated any opportunity to take care of us. My siblings and I were enrolled in school and used convenient public transportation to get around.

Living in a different country with new friends gave me an opportunity I'd never experienced before. I was registered in a mixed high school, and suddenly, I was around boys, a first for me. I loved it! For a sixteen-year-old girl, it was very exciting.

I was popular and happy. My head was full of dreams, and for the first time, I felt comfortable around boys. I made a lot of friends, and after so many years of being kept apart from the other gender, this was thrilling. I realized I was a real female ready to experience life to the fullest.

There had been too much fighting in our old homeland of Morocco, which I certainly didn't miss. Oran was a city full of energy; being there felt more like going to the fair, even though there were dangerous areas in it. As a teenager, this wasn't a big concern to me. My friends and I were more interested in seeing and being seen.

Oran was a beautiful seaside city. The weather was typically warm and sunny. Leafy palm trees graced the streets. The aroma of subtropical flowers filled the air. It was a great place for strolling, full of Old World charm. There were many cafés and shops along the main boulevard. The architecture was European-inspired, and the culture made Oran vibrant and buzzing with energy.

Fort Santa Cruz, first built by the Ottoman Turks and rebuilt by the Spanish, stands majestically on Mount Murdjajo, also known as Pic d'Aidour, 1,300 feet above sea level. There is a magnificent castle and also a massive statue of the Virgin Mary.

I enjoyed sightseeing and people-watching. There was plenty to do that was free: walking on the beach, visiting art galleries, or enjoying an evening promenade. My adaptation to this new lifestyle was amazing.

It didn't take long to make new friends. I didn't miss Morocco and had no regrets. Despite the possible dangers at night, my sixteen-year-old head was full of dreams. I wanted to forget all the bad news of fighting, to put it out of my mind.

We adjusted to the French way of life, eating dinner late at night followed by strolls along city streets where we could see and be seen. At school, boys and girls were discouraged from socializing. So naturally getting to know members of the opposite sex became a huge preoccupation of mine.

Boys hung around shopping malls, cafés, and parks and paraded up and down the boulevards. Of course, girls gravitated to those spots, too. I looked forward to meeting boys, but there was more going on than my hope for romance.

What was going on in Algeria frightened all of us. Riots, bombings, and "freedom fighters" clashing with government forces made it all the more important to have family reassure us. Fortunately, we had many cousins. But one day, a surprise visit by Aunt Rosalie brought disturbing news from Morocco.

Rosalie had traveled by train to speak to my mother about Dad. He'd been arrested and jailed. Conniving as ever, he'd dispatched our aunt to Mom, flush with a generous amount of cash, intent on using his financial influence to help him. Dad always used money to buy people.

Oh, how painful it was to hear my aunt advising Mother that she should return with us to Morocco. Mom was unsure what to do next, but I volunteered to go back and help. My other siblings, though, refused to return.

9

Meeting Bruno

Matters of the heart are often a mystery. Who can explain the "lightning bolt" that strikes so suddenly? When I first saw Bruno, I was immediately drawn to this young man. It was an attraction that haunted my thoughts. Bruno was a star in my eyes. I desperately wanted to be loved by him, but you can't truly love someone you don't yet know.

I had free time after school and spent afternoons visiting my cousins. One day, as I was looking out the window of Françoise's second-floor apartment, I spied a man starting his motorcycle. He was dressed in an air force uniform. I watched him put on his helmet, jump on his rig, and drive away. He didn't see me, but I thought he was delicious!

My heart pounded as I tried to calm myself by taking deep breaths. I needed to meet this handsome man. Teenage lust, chemistry, instant attraction—they all combined to motivate me.

A couple of days later, I spotted Bruno in the parking lot going to his bike. When I walked onto the balcony, he glanced up at me for a few seconds and smiled, melting me. I waved at him, then went back inside the apartment. I was shaking! I didn't know at the time, but I had just met the future father of my two children.

Bruno Marie Fournier was twenty-two years old, a member of the French Air Force based in Toulon, France, and what we called a *pato*, Spanish for "duck." They were called that because they crossed the "duck pond," the Mediterranean Sea. He was often surrounded by other young people, all of whom rode motorcycles. Bruno invited me to come down and meet him and his friends, which was exciting. We drove to the beach, and it was as if time stood still. I was infatuated with the man, and nothing could have stopped us.

Soon we devoted all our free time to going to the beach and getting to know each other. All I wanted was to be with him. We spent as much time together as possible, but I had to hide our relationship from my family. If I got caught, it would have been a big deal. So we learned ways to keep things private.

One day, Bruno crashed his motorcycle and was thrown into a ditch. The accident left him badly scratched and bruised. He asked me to meet him in his apartment. I had to sneak away from home, since my relationship with him was still secret and I knew Mom wouldn't approve.

When I got there, he removed his shirt. I was horrified to see how badly he was hurt. The damage to his back was hard to look at. Part of the muscles had been torn away in the fall. He refused to get help. I did my best to doctor him each day, but it made me ill to look at the wounds. Each day, I brought him food and poured alcohol on his wounds to keep them clean. I could tell it caused him great pain, but he stood still despite the burning effect.

10

Visiting Dad in Prison

Aunt Rosalie wasn't successful in convincing Mom that we should all return to Morocco. Father needed help to get out of jail. However, not one single family member wanted anything to do with him, which was understandable. Nevertheless, I volunteered to go.

My decision was hard because I didn't want to be away from Bruno. Still, I knew someone had to go. Mom needed to keep her job and was legally divorced. Besides, a single woman in Morocco had no voice.

My sister was older but declined to go. Our brother was too young. Furthermore, it was a dangerous time in our part of the world, and we were in the middle of chaos. It felt as if I had no choice, that I was the only logical one to go.

So I was the one who made the trip back to Morocco, traveling by rail with Aunt Rosalie. We didn't talk much. It was my first time being away from my immediate family. I was sad and too upset to face my friends in Morocco. It was humiliating being the one to return.

Dad had several siblings, but they were all upset with him and refused to help. But an uncle agreed to drive me to the prison, a horrible and ancient fort with small windows that smelled of stale urine.

Visitors were divided from the prisoners by screens and sections. There was room for a guard to walk between. My father strode into the room, and his appearance took me by surprise. He was smiling. "I always knew you'd be the one of my three children to help me."

I bristled at the comment. My "help" wasn't out of any great love for this man who had been so cruel to me and my family.

Despite being clean-shaven, he looked awful. Dressed in prison attire, he looked like a criminal! Dad tried to tell me how it was a mistake that he was imprisoned. I heard a woman screaming at him, shouting insults.

"You're a bad man!" she yelled. "Evil scum! I wish my son had never met you." She was accusing my father of involving her son in crooked dealings.

Dad tried to deflect all of this. "Don't listen to that crazy woman," he told me. "She doesn't know what she's talking about."

But I knew his past and how he behaved.

Dad smiled at me, turning on his usual charm. "Janine, I know you can help me. There are some people I need you to speak with."

He instructed me to talk to his attorney and get him help. Dad also wanted me to contact Robert Griguer, one of his loyal friends. "You can trust Robert," he assured me. "We fought together in the war. That makes for strong bonds." Dad knew this man from the Second World War; they had traveled together on a train to fight the Germans in Italy.

When I met with Griguer, he gave me the funds to pay for Dad's attorney as well as the expenses for my trip, which allowed me to stay in Morocco and return to the prison for further visits. The guards always stood near, trying to overhear our conversations. But Dad knew several languages and was smart. He told me to speak with him in Spanish, knowing the guard wouldn't understand.

I didn't make peace with my dad, but I was able to stand up for myself, and he heard my voice without reacting violently.

"You should know I'm not doing this out of any love for you," I told him. "You treated me badly. And not just me but Mother, France, and Alain. So much pain. Don't you realize what it was like? The fear, the hurt, and the sadness it created?"

"Yes, yes, I've been horrible. And I'm sorry. But you're still my daughter, and I do care for you. I need your help. Please, Janine, come back and report to me. I miss you and want to see you again."

At that moment he appeared pitiful, but I visited him three more times.

Dad wanted all of us to return to Morocco. I told him, "Absolutely not! There's no way we're moving back."

All I wanted was to be independent and make my own decisions. I'd grown up in the middle of chaos and learned to find a way—my way! Besides, there was a good-looking air force man back in Oran I wanted to get to know better.

11

About Love

I returned to Oran by myself on a train. This was such an uncertain time, with protests, violence, and fighting seemingly constant. There were many underground groups intent on disruption. It wasn't unusual for there to be militant attacks on buildings and the people in them. We were in the middle of a civil war, with people being executed daily.

But all of this danger didn't deter me from my preoccupation with my new man. When I returned to Oran, I proudly proclaimed to my family that I was in love and had no intention of changing my course. There was only one thing on my mind—Bruno Fournier.

What is this mysterious thing we call *love*? Meeting Bruno, a man to whom I was so attracted, put me into a state of swirling thoughts and feelings. The attraction haunted me.

I was in a bubble of happiness, but it was a bubble that couldn't last. This state of love, or what I thought was love, I'd never experienced before. Naturally, I was unsure how to understand it, to take it all in.

How did I differentiate physical attraction from the *feeling* of love? The physical desire was so strong. But what I was feeling, could it be real love? You can't love what you don't really know. Our physical attraction was powerful, but to take the next step, to go beyond the physical, required getting to know each other in a much more intimate way.

Bruno was a star in my eyes. I wanted to be loved by him. I wanted to have his children. Sadly, Bruno wasn't ready for my kind of relationship, even though I eventually gave him two beautiful children. For him, they were an accident. But for me, I was born to love and be loved, to have children and a loving family.

I was young, and I was a dreamer!

Everything I knew about sex was a guess. No one sat me down and taught me about the human body and the facts of life. I didn't know about hormones and the secrets of childbirth. It was all very mysterious yet exciting!

Mom never mentioned sex. It was as if it didn't exist. Occasionally, she referred to women's genitals as *la boîte d'allumettes*, meaning "a box of matches." "Don't get too close to the fire or your *boîte d'allumettes* will blow up!" she'd say.

That was the limit of Mom's sex education for me. I don't recall any discussion about women's bodies. I tried to ask questions, but sex seemed to be a secret conversation only between adults. Eventually, I went to the library to get a science book and find answers on my own. It was embarrassing.

Since Mom never talked about sex, all I heard from her were warnings that I might become wild like some of the teenagers in our neighborhood who had bad reputations, such as Nellie Hermoso. That was the worst insult!

So we kept watching our "matchboxes!"

When I returned to Oran by myself, I felt stronger and more grown up and had confidence that I'd survive. My siblings and Mom were happy to see me. They were also pleased that I brought enough money from Dad to rent two rooms along with an outside fountain and even an exterior toilet.

I shared one room with my sister, while our mother took the other room. Our brother stayed in the room with Mom. I didn't care at the time about the conditions of the lodging. We had the basics and went with the flow.

However, it wasn't long after I came back that my sister had a fight with Aunt Antoinette. France didn't want to find a job, and my aunt tried to convince her that it was a necessity, but she refused. Instead, France found a group of nuns, the Petites Sœurs des Pauvres, Little Sisters of the Poor, and moved into their convent where she helped them take care of elderly people. She even thought of becoming a nun. It wasn't a bad idea for her to live there, safe from riots and away from family concerns.

Mom then found a room for Alain at an agricultural boarding school in Misserghin, only an hour from the city and run by Catholic monks. He would stay there during the week and return home on weekends or holidays to be with Mom.

Meanwhile, I was enjoying a newfound independence. Together with Bruno and our friends, mainly eight couples who all rode motorcycles, we met at the beach every chance we got. All we wanted to do was make love, have fun, and forget about the fighting all around us.

12

With Child

At first when I got sick, I was convinced I had the flu. For a couple of days, I stayed in bed. Then I talked to my friends, one of whom gave me the name and number of a family doctor. Bruno came with me. He wasn't happy when we discovered I was pregnant, but I was ecstatic. I wanted nothing more than a family and to be a mother.

I didn't tell Mom that I was pregnant, so she was furious when she found out. When I got caught by her on a motorcycle, I was scolded and slapped on the face in front of Bruno, embarrassing me. But I felt bad that I'd upset her so much. It wasn't a good time!

Then more changes happened. Bruno's unit was transferred to a base near Algiers. I stayed behind until he came and spoke to Mom. In French, he asked her for my hand in marriage. They spent time privately, and when they came back, Mother said, "She's too young!"

"I'll watch over her," Bruno replied. "I'm older."

It was a tumultuous time. Thanks to various members of the family, however, we were able to plan a wedding. Mom had custody of us, and thankfully, we didn't hear from Dad. It was Uncle Antoine who gave me away. He was the one who walked me to the church. Bruno and I had already married once in a civil ceremony at the mayor's office. But it was important that we also had a Catholic wedding.

At the time, my uncle had no knowledge of my pregnancy. When he found out later, he was upset. That made me feel bad. I loved and respected him. Looking back, I can see I was making bad choices. But that's sometimes the way of life. I was young and desperate and didn't trust myself.

A cousin of mine, the son of one of my mother's sisters, had recently married. An officer in the French Army, he lived in Algiers with his new wife, which gave me a bit of hope about the future for Bruno and me. The majority of the *pieds-noirs*, ourselves included, could never imagine moving to France.

The day after my wedding, my sister did leave for Algiers. The nuns she'd been staying with arranged for a flight to their convent in France. She lived there for two years without any contact with the rest of our family and was still thinking of becoming a nun.

Meanwhile, Bruno and I were newlyweds and about to embark on our own journey.

13

Blida

Bruno and I relocated to Blida, about twenty-eight miles from Algiers. We moved into a room rented from an old lady who was raising two of her grandchildren, both under six years of age. It was good for me to spend time around children.

In 1960, Blida was a town with French character but divided between French and Arab quarters. It was surrounded by orchards. Merchants traded in oranges and flour. There was also some light manufacturing. The climate in Blida was warm, and unlike Algiers, it was safer to go out in the evenings after sunset.

I wasn't able to go anywhere alone. All day I waited for Bruno. To occupy my time, I learned to do tricot, a kind of warp knitting. We didn't have much money, but enough to buy yarn to make outfits for our baby.

One day, out of the blue, I received a letter from my father. To my dismay, he wrote that he was coming to meet my husband. I was in great shock at this news. How was he going to feel about Bruno, or, for that matter, what would Bruno's reaction be when he met my father?

Dad must have done his prison time. Now he was ready to mess with our lives. I knew all too well I couldn't trust my father. Of course, I didn't want him around my new family. But it was more than not wanting him to interfere; I was ashamed of him.

I kept lying to cover up the truth about him. It was just so hard to admit to others what kind of man my father was.

Dad arrived and checked into a local hotel. He seemed to be in a positive mood to meet Bruno. At the same time, he was playing the sympathy card about how we'd left him in Morocco. *Poor old me* was his tone!

He complained about how I was a wild girl making bad decisions. Well, he was right about that. I knew it, but I wasn't going to admit it to him. It made me furious when he told me he'd pressed charges against the mayor of the village where Bruno and I had wed. He said it should have been him walking me down the aisle. I was glad he hadn't, and I wanted him to go away.

How could Dad be so vain? He was no longer a father figure for me, but a clown. All those years of torturing us with his violence. Now he had the nerve to try to manipulate my husband. He couldn't stand to see me happy. So he tried to get Bruno to doubt me. Dad told him things, placing me in a negative light and attempting to adversely influence him. *Mettre la puce à l'oreille*, which in French means "to put a flea in the ear." In other words, Dad was hoping to convince Bruno that I wasn't good for him.

Bruno was all ears and smiled when Dad told him I was ungrateful and wild. He knew better than to trust my father. Still, I didn't really know Bruno, and he didn't know me. I was only seventeen years old and crying for acceptance. I just wanted to be loved. We were like two strangers. I hadn't talked much about my father, so meeting him was a challenge for Bruno.

14

My Son is Born

My pregnancy was pretty normal, but I had no idea how I was going to give birth. I went to see a local doctor who gave me an idea of what to expect. Fortunately, it was enough information for me. Of course, women have been giving birth for millennia—typically, with the help passed on by elders, family members, and those trained in childbirth.

I gave birth to my son, Bruno Jean Pierre Fournier, in the local hospital of Blida, Algeria, on May 8, 1961. It was a primitive hospital by today's standards but advanced enough to perform the surgery to deliver him by Cesarean section. I woke up sometimes during the night to be rolled and cleaned and was in and out of consciousness but heard my name being called. For the operation, I'd been put to sleep with gas, so waking up was slow.

Then there was my husband facing me and telling me the baby was healthy. He brought him to my bed and placed him across my chest. My beautiful newborn! He was a big baby, and a nurse took him from room to room to show him off.

Later, I woke up in a large room of twenty-five beds filled with sick patients. They were all Muslim country ladies. The community hospital was basic, but all that mattered to me was that my baby boy was healthy. And we were well taken care of, given good food, and treated with kindness by some of the sweetest people I've ever known.

15

Fighting All Around

During this time, riots, bombings, and violence were still all around us. The country was in terrible turmoil. The news drove us crazy. Everyone was horribly agitated.

We were planning to return to Oran when Bruno informed me that he wasn't going to enlist for another term in the French Air Force. He didn't want to renew his contract with the military. Furthermore, his superiors didn't believe the military was for him. Naturally, this worried me greatly. How would he provide for us? We had our first fight that day.

When we did return to Oran, we moved in with Mother and Alain. Mom had good recommendations from her work in Rabat and had been rehired at the military hospital. She helped and provided for us when she could. But we had to continue finding ways to survive financially.

Bruno took a job with Uncle Antoine in his mechanic shop. My husband's training had been working on airplanes, but he was happy to start with my uncle on cars. I found a job as a hostess at a movie theater.

Theaters were popular and an incredible distraction from the worries and troubles of daily life. They also provided the news in pictures, shown in newsreel reports before the film at a time when many people, including us, didn't have a television.

My job at the theater was to guide customers with my flashlight to their seats. We lived on tips, but it was easy money. Although I was working, I still had my responsibilities as a new mother. Bruno was only three months old at this time. Alain watched him while I was at work and brought the baby to me so I could breastfeed him.

Meanwhile, the situation in the country worsened daily. Without a television, we got news on the radio. Things were getting bloody, which didn't bode well for our situation.

The OAS continued to oppose those who wanted independence from the French. Bombings and targeted assassinations happened both in France and Algeria. From April 1961 to April 1962, there were an estimated 2,000 deaths due to the violence.

Attempts were made on the life of Charles de Gaulle, the French president, as well as on the prominent philosopher Jean-Paul Sartre, who supported the FLN. Some French generals attempted a coup. Tanks were parked in front of the French Parliament, and a machine gun was posted in the salon of the presidential palace. The French government declared a state of emergency. The coup failed, and de Gaulle retained power. But after years of resistance and revolution, it appeared Algerian independence was finally going to happen.

A dark event, the Oran massacre of 1962, happened over three days in July. There were mass killings of *pied-noir* and European expatriates living in Algeria by members of the FLN. Estimates range from ninety-five to 365 people being killed.

Moving to France was becoming a reality. We might have been *pieds-noirs*, but we were also French citizens protected by the Évian Accords. It was time to leave Algeria, so in 1961, Bruno, our baby, and I headed to Marseille in France.

PART THREE
France

16

Marseille and Toulon

The next five years were the most difficult of my life, a period when I experienced significant struggles. Still, one can always find some joy, something positive, even during times like that, but often it takes some real digging. I'm sure those years made me a stronger person, but today it isn't joyful to reminisce about that time in my life.

Bruno and I were grateful to escape with our lives, but we were thrust into another situation of having to find a place to live and make ends meet. We landed in Marseille after making a noisy and terrifying journey in the belly of a cargo plane. The French Air Force flew in several planes to evacuate families and deliver them to safety. Most of these people had never experienced this kind of air transport unless they were in the military.

Marseille is a beautiful port city in France. At its heart is the Vieux-Port. The centuries-old Fort Saint-Jean stands in the Vieux-Port near the Romanesque-style Saint-Laurent Church. Down by the water is a lively yacht marina and many stylish hotels, waterfront cafés, and seafood restaurants that have made this city a popular tourist destination. The streets fill at night with pedestrians out for a stroll or to enjoy the bars and club life.

Of course, we cared little about all that during this stressful time. What concerned me most was the safety of my baby. Desperately, I wanted a better life for my precious boy. I loved being a mother and breastfeeding him. When he was hungry, I opened my shirt and brought him close to me. That was special!

When we reached Toulon, I met Bruno's family. My husband's parents were the sweetest couple. They had five children: three girls and two boys, including, of course, Bruno. I'd never been told much about them, but we hugged, smiled, and reassured one another that all would be well.

What I didn't know prior to our arrival was that Bruno wasn't on speaking terms with his parents. Nothing had been said in front of me, but it didn't take long for me to see my mother-in-law getting agitated when talking with her son.

For myself, I got along fine with Bruno's family. In fact, I eventually became his mother's confidante. Her stories of how she and her family succeeded after the men went off to fight during the Second World War fascinated me. They were a conservative and very religious Catholic family, but Bruno wasn't either of those things. Perhaps that was the source of some of the tension between them.

We baptized our son. Several times after that, I was told to go to church. My siblings and I had been baptized Catholics as infants, but we never attended Sunday school. I was too embarrassed to tell them that I was unable to understand the Mass.

I was very impressed with my father-in-law's gardening skills. He was adept at growing wonderful plants. The yard was about one acre, and he used every inch to grow fruit and vegetables. My admiration of his garden was strong, and I asked many questions. He taught me some things that paid off later in my life.

The first thing he instructed me on was to separate the trash and recycle the waste. Anyone familiar with growing plants soon learns the value of composting. He had other lessons, too, which increased my appreciation of gardening, something that has stayed with me to this day.

On Sunday nights, we had soup. Bruno's mother—we called her Mamie—made the best *poule au pot*, "chicken in a pot," using the amazing fresh vegetables such as cabbage and carrots from her husband's garden. She'd undoubtedly learned her cooking skills as a result of growing up in the mostly agricultural region of Limousin in south-central France. I loved that woman and her cooking!

Politics were on everybody's lips, but I'd had enough of that talk and learned to keep my mouth shut when surrounded by French people who had dealt with too much death. Thousands of young men had died in war, too many in vain. The people of France were sickened and tired of all that. And I believed they were scared of us. I kept hearing among them how too many of their boys had been sent to fight and die in Algeria. I didn't dare bring up that subject, was tired of all the violence, and just wanted love and peace.

So instead I turned my attention to cooking. It was my favorite subject, and Mamie was a good teacher. This experience, much like learning gardening from Bruno's father, greatly benefited me later in life.

While living with Bruno's parents in Toulon, I started getting sick in the mornings. It didn't take long, just a week later, to learn I was pregnant again. We kept the news to ourselves.

Bruno and I both got jobs to help pay the bills. Then one day, Bruno had a fight with his mom. It must have been a bad one because she asked him to leave. We didn't own a car, so off we went on foot. We walked for several hours, pushing our baby carriage, and eventually reached the home of Bruno's sister, Jeanne. She was married to André, and they were kind enough to take us in.

The family dynamics were complicated, and I didn't understand them. I was an outsider, but I did my best to fit in with French manners. However, I didn't feel well and only wanted a comfortable place for the three of us.

This was a time of confusion regarding my feelings about my husband. Bruno was often unhappy and cold toward me. It was disconcerting and made me feel disoriented. In order to distract myself from these troubling thoughts, I spent time with Mamie in Coste Chaude. She was a good woman. Her country home was built during the time of Napoleon Bonaparte. Here she raised chickens, and my job was to retrieve eggs from the nests. To this very day, I love doing that. It seems that I was born to be a farmer.

Bruno and I were able to find a small apartment on the other side of Toulon, but it was nothing special. Our son, Bruno Junior, was only thirteen months old and still in cloth diapers. The landlord was an older lady who lived in an apartment above us with her husband and mature son. She was as mean as a cobra. When she found out I was a *pied-noir* and pregnant, she treated me harshly. Since my husband was French, he got along with her, but he'd never mentioned to her that I was expecting another child. Already she was complaining that our baby boy was keeping her awake at night, but she never said anything to my husband, just me. Making matters worse, she only allowed me to use the washing basins in the courtyard two days a week, which became a real problem, since I needed to wash diapers.

My second pregnancy was uncomfortable, and I spent a lot of time in bed. I didn't like living in France, especially with our difficulties. I was eight months pregnant when it came time to give birth and I had to have another Cesarean. My baby girl, Murielle, was born in a private clinic in Toulon. After giving birth, I was ill and very weak, so much so that my mother-in-law asked me to come back to her home. I was so grateful. What a grace! She was a great help in putting me back on my feet.

Mamie nursed me with a mixture of egg yolks, brandy, and honey. It was good to drink, and I loved the effect of the alcohol. It was enough to make me drowsy, and then I could take naps.

Shortly after Murielle was born, Alain arrived on a refugee boat. We stretched some mattresses on the kitchen floor for him. It was the best we could do in our cramped quarters. But he was a big help with my baby.

When Bruno and I had left Oran, Mom was still working at the military hospital. The other family members who had moved to France told us the news from Algeria, which was horrifying. Then, at long last, Mom was able to leave Algeria. One of the last Europeans to get out of the country, she escaped by jumping onto the deck of a ship full of refugees, all of whom were running for their lives. The crowded vessel made people push and panic. They were angry and fearful after just escaping the desperate situation in Algeria where people were being slaughtered like animals. Decapitation was the most common form of execution. Algeria was no longer French and certainly not safe for anyone of French descent.

We were so relieved to get my mother back. We had no phone and no way to know what was happening to her. But she was alive and out of Algeria, escaping with just a blanket, a bag, and a small suitcase full of baby clothes. My fierce mother had saved the clothes, determined to bring them to her new granddaughter. What a relief when she knocked on our door. We were together again and all safe.

The arrival of Mom in France was a happy occasion, but our living quarters were very crowded, and now we were making room for another mattress. We had no idea what to do next. It was a dilemma. Mom was with us now. Brother Alain, too. Shortly after she arrived from Oran, my mother made a trip to Paris and convinced France to leave the convent and come live with us. So now there was Bruno, me, baby Bruno, and Murielle, along with Mom, Alain, and eventually France—too many people in too small a space.

We bought the newspaper each day and searched for jobs. My husband was already working, but he was also very controlling. He managed our money and ruled my life. Although Mom was happy to be somewhere she could relax after years of turbulence, a storm was brewing in my marriage.

Things were tense as well with our landlady. One afternoon, Mom and I were sitting and chatting when I heard the landlady talking. She was standing next to our kitchen window, speaking with her adult son. We became silent in order to listen to them better.

"Have you heard that baby wailing in the night?" the landlady asked her son. "There's no sleeping with all that noise."

That angered me, and I got up, walked to the front door, and confronted her. "Stop your complaining!"

Her son approached me and yelled, "This apartment is too small for so many people!"

I argued with him, and when he came even closer in a threatening manner, I panicked, grabbed a broom, and smacked him in the face. When I saw he was bleeding, I knew I'd made a big mistake.

17

On the Move Again

Bruno was offered another job selling and working on cars, and once again, we moved, this time into the first of a series of hotels. It was several hours away from our old apartment and far from our mean landlady, which was fine by me. Still, things were tight. We needed another income and a babysitter. Nevertheless, we did manage, but just barely. At least we didn't starve.

Through a friend, we found help to watch our children. She was an older lady who lived in the country with her adolescent daughter and agreed to watch our children during the week. It was a safer arrangement for the little ones, since we had to roam from hotel to hotel.

I found a job at a clothing store and made some new friends. Then a better job came my way: the owner of a nightclub hired me as a waitress. The pay was more, and we certainly needed the money. This job kept our hotel bills paid. However, I was only nineteen and too young to be working there. I didn't tell them, and honestly, I don't think they cared.

The money at the club was good, but some of the clientele were shady. I was offered another kind of employment that would pay more. I could have been a madame, and I would have been a good one. Just kidding! I knew it was illegal and was aware of what was happening. It was bad enough that my father had taught me criminal ways when I was younger, training me even to break the law. I didn't want to go down that road. What I really needed was Mom and my family. Even though the money was great at the club, I told Bruno I was going home to my mother. I walked away from that world with no regrets. My children needed me, and I needed them. I wanted to be a mother they'd be proud of. So I took the train to Paris to be with Mom.

After the argument with the mean landlady in the tiny, cramped apartment, my mother had also decided to leave. She got a job working at a military hospital in Paris, much like the ones before in Morocco and Algeria, found a place in Quincy-sous-Sénart just outside the capital, and took Alain and France to live with her.

18

Quincy-sous-Sénart and Cannes

It was 1963, and Mom was able to have my children and me live with her in Quincy-sous-Sénart, thanks to her new job at the military hospital in Paris. However, the only transportation from there to her work was a train that took about an hour each way. Still, it was a relief to have something like a normal life once again. We were busy and poor but happy. Life was good with no more war. We'd all been through enough terror and had witnessed too many atrocities.

Bruno didn't accompany us on our move to Paris; he joined us later. We hadn't been getting along and needed a break from each other. So I turned my attention to my children and to my mother.

It was a few months before Mom was able to rent an apartment in Paris. In the meantime, we stayed at the place she rented in Quincy-sous-Sénart. She had also reconnected with a good friend she'd met while working at the Oran military hospital. They had become a couple, and my half-brother, Richard, was born in 1964. Although Mom loved her friend, they never married. He was Jewish, and I believed she was too traumatized concerning everything Jews had endured in Morocco. Also, in those days people normally didn't have mixed marriages. We were a Catholic family, and Mom wasn't inclined to break rules. The Moguel clan, though, voiced its disapproval.

Mom's rental house was in the middle of an apple orchard and was owned by a French nobleman who used it as a hunting lodge. It was a quaint but older place. We had to keep a fire always going in the fireplace in the colder months, since it was the only source of heat. In the kitchen, we cooked on a wood stove and had a pot hanging in the chimney so there was always soup for the family. I don't remember not having food.

The location of our new home was withheld from Dad. So it was a surprise one day when he showed up at our door unexpectedly. He had moved to Spain and was as resourceful as ever. So, of course, he'd discovered where we were living. He wasn't invited to meet with us at Mom's place, so instead we got together several times at a café in the village.

Dad's big smile never fooled me, but he did have an intriguing proposal. He offered to move us to the south of France into a house in Cannes. The owner was an older woman who lived half the year in Spain, and Dad was willing to let us live there until we found another place. For me and my family, this was a good solution. It would literally get us out of the cold. I had a little money saved and decided to accept his proposition. Mom was more cautious and warned, "Be careful of any of your father's shady deals. You know him. He's crooked!"

Of course, I knew all too well how Dad operated. But he'd bought and sold real estate in Morocco and had several properties in Rabat. I wasn't really surprised by his offer, though I was wary of his motives. Still, who wouldn't want to live on the Côte d'Azur, the French Riviera, with all its luxurious charm sprinkled with the awesome beaches of Saint-Tropez, Cannes, and Villefranche-sur-mer?

So Bruno and I left Quincy-sous-Sénart and moved to Cannes with our children. Bruno Senior had joined me and the kids in Mom's house and was thrilled to relocate to the south of the country. What wasn't there to love about beautiful weather in a paradise of aristocrats, artists, and the jet set! Bruno knew the ways of the people there—the accents, food, and culture—which made the transition easier. However, it wasn't long, just a couple of months later, when we were told the owner was returning from Spain. We contacted a real estate agent, found a modern apartment within walking distance of the beach, and looked forward with hope to the future.

One day, my father introduced us to a new lady friend. Her name was Deedee; at least that was what he called her. Pretty, blond, and in her mid-forties, she seemed like a good companion for him. They were together each time I saw Dad. But I wanted to know more about her. Alain was now a teenager and had been visiting them. He spent time with Deedee, and when he saw me, I asked a lot of questions about her: "What's she like? Who is she? Does she have any children?" I wanted to know what my father was up to!

After one of our visits, Alain confided to me that Deedee had told him the police were asking her questions about Dad's dealings. It seemed he was up to his old illegal tricks, and suspicions had been raised.

We'd been living in Cannes for a couple of years when a friend mentioned that Canada was offering immigration, and if people qualified, the country paid all expenses. Bruno became very excited. One Christmas, when he was a teen, he'd received a book about trapping and living in a cabin in Canada. From that time on, he'd dreamed of a land of wide-open spaces full of adventure. Canada—the last frontier!

We thought hard about this opportunity. Eventually, we agreed this was something to pursue. When we applied, all four of us were accepted. We decided to keep our plans secret from Dad. He was spending his time between Spain and France and was still very much under suspicion by the authorities.

It was 1966, and a new chapter was about to begin for Bruno Senior, Bruno Junior, Murielle, and me in Canada.

PART FOUR
Canada

19

O Canada!

Our time in France was coming to an end. Everyone was nervous but also very excited. A new frontier in Canada awaited us!

It wouldn't be easy to leave Mother behind, but in many ways the timing was perfect. Dad was in trouble with the law again. It was terrifying. I was afraid we'd be dragged into his web of intrigue and knew we had to separate ourselves from him, to get away to somewhere different, someplace that would be difficult for him to track us down.

Mom invited us to stay with her at her rue Championnet apartment in Paris's Eighteenth Arrondissement until we left for Canada. She wanted to protect us. Although I hadn't seen Dad for a couple of months, I had the sickening feeling he'd soon be caught by the authorities. Mom and Bruno Senior did their best to keep the bad news about my father from me, but the suspicion was still there, strong like a premonition.

For the first time in my life, I had hope that we'd escape Dad once and for all. He'd followed us since the day we'd left Morocco. So we packed our bags, grabbed the children, and made our getaway to Mom's apartment.

At the time, France and Alain didn't share my concerns about Dad. They seemed to have a newfound friendship with our father and had been visiting him. He'd been giving them gifts, which seemed funny to me. My sister had never been close to him and, in fact, had avoided him. Alain was finally forming a closer bond with Dad, and I was glad for that. But I knew Dad couldn't be trusted. I worried for my siblings, but my first responsibility was to myself and my children.

I'd never been happy living in France, so going to Canada was the best thing that could happen to us. The grass was always greener on the other side, as the saying went, and for Bruno and me, being young and adventurous made us ready to face the future.

I knew very little about Canada. We got a map of that large country along with a couple of books from the library. I spent hours looking through the pictures and dreaming about the beautiful open spaces, the abundance of wild animals, and the canoeing on emerald lakes. I became obsessed with the mountains, lakes, and lush wilderness. My children were young but thrilled as we told them about bears, wolves, and all the other wildlife.

Bruno procured plane tickets for the four of us, we updated our passports, and everyone had a medical checkup. France, Alain, and our half-brother, Richard, shared Mother's last meal with us before the trip.

Mother trusted me, and I reassured her that I'd do whatever it took to make a great life for my children. She reminded me that in France my children and I would always have a home. I thought about that every time I encountered an obstacle in my journey. It empowered me to know that no matter what happened, as long as Mom was alive, I could return home.

20

Arrival in Montreal

It was mid-March 1966 when we flew to Montreal. We were relocating to Quebec, which the French-speaking residents called *la belle province*, or "the beautiful province." For many people, it represented something similar to the American dream.

It was a rainy day in Paris when we left the airport, but in my heart the sun was shining. Three flight attendants tiptoed around us, flashing radiant smiles while serving beverages and delicious food. They were young and friendly and told us to expect big changes: "Be prepared for ice and snow up to May. The winters last six months, but Canadians love the snow and go outdoors every chance they get."

They gave us other words of advice: "Quebec is French-speaking, but it is *not* France. Don't try to impose your culture or try to change them." They mentioned the French-Canadian accent, which was often mocked in France. The dialect they used had many old French words in it. Nevertheless, the Québécois had the same *joie de vivre*, the joy of living, that the French in France had.

As we flew over the Atlantic Ocean, we peered out of the little windows in the plane but could only see clouds. After many hours, we were over Montreal, and I could see that it was a big city covered with snow. I had never really seen so much snow before and it made me think of Christmas cards. So beautiful!

When we finally landed at Dorval Airport, a big sign greeted us: BIENVENUE À MONTRÉAL, QUÉBEC, LA BELLE PROVINCE. Looking at the snow, I realized we didn't have coats warm enough for the freezing temperatures. But we were well received by the Canadian immigration officials, who gave us our first taste of a dynamic and endearing culture. I was grateful for their kindness and warmth. We were offered boots for our children along with a place to stay for a couple of days. An appointment was also made to meet the officials on Monday.

Once outside the airport terminal, the air was so cold that it was hard to breathe. It was mid-afternoon when we arrived by taxi at a boarding house. The car pulled up to the front of the building and dropped us off. We were exhausted and in need of a good rest.

The spacious bathroom in the boarding house was bigger than I was used to. It was wonderful to shower and feel the hot water. In France, that was a costly commodity, so I reveled in the luxury.

Much refreshed, we left to go to dinner, but when we returned, we were dismayed to discover someone had come into our room and searched our belongings. I panicked and walked outside to get help, telling the person at the boarding house office what had happened. We were obviously upset and asked for another room. Unfortunately, that couldn't be accommodated, so we had to stay where we were, nervous and on guard.

We had exactly $250 left to our name. Fortunately, Bruno had kept the cash in his wallet or that might have been taken, as well. Dejectedly, I picked up our clothes scattered all over the room. We were tired from the trip, and everyone fell asleep as soon as we put our heads on the pillows.

A few days before leaving France, I'd answered a knock on the door of my mother's place. Two young men stood there. They introduced themselves, and I knew from their accents that they were Americans. The two men were Mormons going door to door to talk to people about Jehovah. I was curious and wanted to learn more. When I mentioned we were moving to Montreal, they encouraged me to look up the Mormon church there.

So now we were in Montreal, and the next morning was Sunday. Why not check out the Mormon church? We hired a taxi and went there for a service. A nicer group of people I'd never met. They welcomed us and made us feel like family.

One of the first things we needed to do was find employment. While still in France, we'd learned that Canada was very welcoming to young men and women willing to work in the restaurant-and-food industry, which was anxious to hire waitresses, cooks, and pastry chefs. That presented a fine opportunity for me!

I applied for a job at La Crêpe Bretonne, a new restaurant on Rue de la Montagne in downtown Montreal, initially as a server, later becoming a waitress. The owner was French and from France. It was easy employment, and I fitted right in. The food was great, and everything being French, the music and the atmosphere made the place feel very familiar.

I loved crêpes, so working there was a bonus. The crêpes were very large, paper-thin, and cooked on a hot stone grill until golden brown on one side. The fillings were almost any kind that could be imagined. Then they were folded over like envelopes and served hot with jugs of local maple syrup. My favorite crêpe had apples and cheese in it.

The restaurant's French onion soup was legendary and was baked in earthenware pots and served overflowing with cheese. I've often wanted to return to that establishment but was disappointed to hear that it had closed down years ago. Perhaps such things are best left to fond memories, since those only get richer with time.

My initial impression of French Canadians was that they were both fun and kind. I knew right away I was with my people. Although they spoke French, they were often difficult to understand. Their dialect, slang, and expressions could be a problem. But I'd lived in several countries and was used to the need to adapt to new surroundings.

French Canadians have a sweet demeanor, which instantly inspired confidence in us. We discovered that it was easy to be promoted at work if you learned to be kind and quiet. The Québécois considered the French from France a little naughty and critical. I totally agreed: you never messed with the French!

In Montreal, I picked up Quebec expressions and even imitated their tone, just as I had in France when I was concerned about my North African accent. And I kept my mouth shut, always smiled, and quickly mastered being a good waitress at La Crêpe Bretonne.

The restaurant was inside a large building in the center of the city and was a happy place full of students and other young people. The owner was a Monsieur Thaven from France, who was very demanding and worked us like cattle. But it only took me a week to get to know the menu and keep the customers moving. I found it fairly easy and was always pleased when after the patrons got up from their tables, they left quarters under the plates for tips. This was good and welcome money needed to help with our expenses.

Bruno Senior was hired at a local garage specializing in French Renault vehicles. But he never shared his income with me, and his wages weren't enough to support our family. We needed a second income.

Montreal is actually a city built on the largest of the 234 islands of the Hochelaga Archipelago at the confluence of two rivers, the St. Lawrence and the Ottawa, in southwestern Quebec. The location of Montreal proved to be vastly important and contributed to the city's development into a major hub for transportation and commerce.

For us, daily living in Montreal was very different from what we'd experienced in France. The standard working hours were 8:00 a.m. to 4:00 p.m., which allowed lots of time for leisure activities. We discovered shopping along with many outdoor activities. Ice hockey was huge in Canada, and people had a great passion for the sport. I found everything in Montreal a welcome relief from the hustle and bustle of France. The lifestyle allowed me to live with far less stress.

Mount Royal is a great destination for Montreal's residents. It boasts year-round activities from jogging, hiking, biking, picnicking, and concerts in the summer, to tubing, snowshoeing, and skating in the winter. It's a fabulous place in the middle of the city, and I enjoyed its beautiful scenery. This magnificent urban green space was designed by Frederick Law Olmstead, famous for his design of Central Park in New York City.

A must-see place for anyone coming to Montreal, Mount Royal was the best place to relax and spend time in nature, something necessary for all of us. It was certainly helpful to me. There are many paths and trails to wander and even Lac aux Castors, an artificial lake and a refuge for humans as well as many animals and birds. From Mount Royal's terrace, the entire city's panorama can be viewed. It's easy to spend an entire day there, and if hungry or thirsty, plenty of food and beverages are available.

JANINE WINTERS

Being outside is something most Canadians enjoy, and Montrealers are extremely active people. Plenty of people walk their dogs on the mountain. As a big dog lover, I particularly appreciated a big park with lots of grass.

21

Excitement and Stress

I was excited about being in Canada. It was a big country with lots of possibilities for us to live free from some of the stress and strife I'd experienced nearly all my life. And living among the French-speaking Québécois made it easier to adjust. But I soon discovered that Canada had its own political strife.

For the most part, French Canadians had kept their distinct cultural tastes and values. A strong Roman Catholic influence dating back to early colonial times and the Jesuit missionaries had something to do with that. In 1960, the Liberal Party came to power in Quebec and ushered in a more modern secular approach to the economic and educational system. That marked the end of the social and political power of the Catholic Church, but there was still the tradition of large families and marrying within their own community for many French Canadians.

There was a certain tension between the English and French, and in the 1970s, there were growing nationalist aspirations for a greater recognition of equality and freedom for the Québécois. Some wanted a separate country.

I wanted no part of this. Politics had never interested me, and I'd already lived through enough of the kind of conflict that came with violent revolution for independence. It reminded me too much of what had occurred in Morocco and Algeria, and it scared me to see people turning on one another. I was seeking peace and feared an encounter with the nightmare of war again. Instead, I focused on the good in life, spending my time with friends and my children. These were the important things, something I'd learned by from living through hard times.

It wasn't easy to make ends meet. Finances were always on my mind. Bruno was very private and distant, which made me feel more responsible for our children. I could tell he wasn't happy with me and clearly had other interests outside his wife and children.

Although he was hired to work at a garage, he kept his earnings in a private account in his name only. He called it "saving for our old days," but I really think he was saving for *his* old days! That just fed my distrust of him. He was becoming less of a husband and more of a mystery.

With no car, we had to rely on public transportation. We looked for an apartment close to work. Fortunately, we found one within walking distance, about a half mile from La Crêpe Bretonne. It was small, a studio with just two bedrooms, but it met our needs and was a place we could afford.

I couldn't count on my husband for security, though I wanted him to accompany me on my walks home from work. I didn't feel safe, and he knew it could be dangerous for a woman to walk alone at night. However, Bruno worked during the day and then went out in the evenings to distract himself. I didn't see him much during the week, and when he got the children on the weekend, he took them to Mount Royal to enjoy the outdoors.

It got to the point where I had no desire to spend time with Bruno. He totally turned me off! I thought he was cruel, mean, cold, and unhappy. Although he never physically attacked me, he gave me the cold shoulder and silent treatment. As partners, we didn't fit anymore. I wanted to run, but I had my children and loved being a mother. Certainly, I couldn't afford to stop working, so I had to compromise with their father.

I knew our marriage was in trouble. Still young, I was a very unhappy woman working twelve hours per day six days per week and spending all my income on our expenses. We had made this big move to Canada, and now it was becoming clear that Bruno wasn't the man I thought he was when we first fell in love. I wished I could talk to my mom, but we didn't have a phone. Besides, it was quite expensive to call France.

We settled for writing each other cards and letters. Mom remained quiet about the problems with my dad. I knew she just wanted to protect me, to shield me from any bad news.

22

A New Friend

One day, a letter came from my brother, Alain. He'd gone to the Canadian embassy in Paris and had decided it was time to move from France and live in Canada. I was thrilled he'd be joining us! Bruno, however, wasn't, which brought another area of contention between us.

Bruno always showed anger when my brother was around. I couldn't understand why he treated him like that. It was painful for me to watch. I loved my little brother, and we were always close. Dad had treated him badly, and I felt protective of him.

I think I craved someone close to me I could talk with. It would have been nice to have my brother here. Or even to meet someone, a new friend with whom I could really talk. Soon, to my joy, that happened.

Since Bruno and I were both working so much during the week, we had to hire a sitter to watch the children. Searching the newspaper ads, I found a family willing to watch them. It was our hope to get someone close. There was only so much time in the day, and I relied on public transportation to get to and from work.

My only day off was Sunday, which I spent much of doing laundry so the children had clean clothes for the week. Then I prepared their suitcases and made sure everything was ready. Meanwhile, Bruno was responsible for taking care of the children during the weekend. More and more, it was as if we lived separate lives.

One Sunday, I went down to the basement to use the washer and dryer, and as I read a book to pass the time, I heard some people walking down the stairs. A woman entered holding a small child and accompanied by two little boys, who appeared about the same age as Bruno Junior and Murielle. She glanced around and said something to her boys in French.

"*Bonjour, madame,*" I said to her.

She looked at me with surprise. "Are you French?"

"Yes, I'm French from Morocco."

She smiled and said in English, "I can't understand the French-Canadian accent."

I agreed it wasn't easy. She introduced herself as Josée Lupuyo and told me she was married to a man named Jacky. They were the parents of the two boys. Josée was babysitting the child in her arms.

"Can I help you with the little one while you fill your washing machine?" I asked her.

"That would be very kind of you."

As we put her laundry into a machine, we began a long conversation about our families. It turned out we had a lot in common. She was twenty-seven and young like me. Both of us had experienced difficult childhoods.

"My grandparents raised me after my mother was found dead on the train tracks," she told me. "They were poor and already getting on in years when my mother died, but they did their best to raise me and my younger sister. I was born in a small village in southeastern France and never traveled far from there when I was younger."

I was curious about the circumstances of her mother's death but reluctant to probe that wound any further.

Although Josée was shy, I could tell she was very proud of her French heritage. The French were apprehensive in the company of foreigners and often compensated for it by giving the impression they knew everything. However, Josée wasn't as bad in that way as many of her countrymen and women.

Like me, her childhood was rough. She carried a lot of sadness and pain around with her. Here was someone I could comfort and with whom I could share my own experiences. This had turned out to be my lucky day—I had a new best friend!

That night, I was all fired up when I saw Bruno and the children. He could be picky about new people but agreed to meet Josée's husband, Jacky, along with their two sons.

I invited the Lupuyos over for hot chocolate and French apple pie. When Bruno met Jacky, he was pleasantly surprised. They hit it off immediately and gave each other hugs and kisses the way Frenchmen did.

Jacky told Bruno, "I got a job as a welder here. I heard there's a lot of construction and industrial work going on in the city."

"That's great!" exclaimed Bruno. "I'm a mechanic myself. We might end up working on the same projects."

"That would be great!" Jacky replied. "It's always good to have skilled professionals from different trades working together."

Bruno was enjoying this conversation. "Absolutely! So, have you had a chance to explore Paris yet?"

And on and on they chatted, immediately becoming fast friends.

It was good they liked each so much, probably because they both came from France, because it helped my friendship with Josée. We were like family.

Our integration into Canadian life became easier with friends. From that first meeting with the Lupuyos, we enjoyed one another's company and started doing everything together. Our husbands spent the weekends with our children doing outdoor activities, which gave Josée and me time to explore supermarkets and discover Canadian food. It wasn't always easy for us to make new connections with strangers, but the friendly nature of the Québécois helped us to feel more comfortable in our new land.

We lived just a few floors away from our new friends' apartment and kept in touch daily. I have often asked myself how my life would have been different if I hadn't been there in the basement that day. Josée and I became very close, and she was proud to be my friend, introducing me to others as her sister. She was generous and kind, made me feel secure, and was the first person I called on when I needed support. This total kindness was a blessing between us; I miss her and hope she's watching me in spirit.

Josée was too shy to work with the public and got annoyed when she didn't understand the locals. She was also upset that her husband didn't earn enough to take care of their family. Like me, she needed to work to have enough money to support everyone.

Unfortunately, she'd never traveled much or ever had a job except to immigrate to Canada. I, on the other hand, had lived in three other countries and dodged bullets! Because I was strong and able, I took Josée under my wing and helped her realize she had what it took to learn how to make a living. Nothing was insurmountable, and I found it enriching to help her.

We both faced the same problem of the need to work but also to find a reliable babysitter. I began asking other waitresses if they knew of anyone and searched for opportunities my new friend might be able to do.

Soon Josée got her first job—checking coats for customers in a fancy restaurant. As guests came in with coats, she hung them up in the cloakroom and gave them tickets. When the patrons were ready to leave, they returned their tickets; she gave back their garments and received generous tips.

The work was easy, and since she was only there for dinnertime, it was ideal for her situation. Plus, working outside her home and mixing with the locals broke the ice for her. She was able to develop more confidence interacting with the public.

23

Big Changes

When Bruno and I arrived in Montreal in March 1966, the city was busy preparing for Expo 67. The world's fair was a very big deal and was coming here! At the time, we had no idea what a change that would make to our lives.

From the start, it wasn't going to be easy. A great deal of work went into getting the city ready for such a major exhibition. Workers were engaged in construction around the clock. While this was to be a great opportunity for Montreal to project a new and better image to the world, it was also going to have an enormous economic impact on everyone there, including us.

Originally, the Soviet Union had won the right to host the event in Moscow. It wanted to celebrate the fiftieth anniversary of its revolution. However, the Soviets decided in 1962 that the fair would be too costly and had concerns about security, so it backed out and the world's fair went to Montreal for 1967.

Jean Drapeau, the mayor of Montreal, had a grand vision. He wanted a big party to showcase the beauty of Quebec and celebrate 100 years of Canada's Confederation, while also highlighting the food and cultures of the planet's nations.

Montreal had a bad reputation that Drapeau wanted to change. At one time, the city was known as the sex capital of North America, full of alcohol and prostitutes. With the help of a US public-relations company, the mayor was determined to create a new image that would present Montreal as an international city, similar to Paris. Expo 67 would be the ticket to turn the metropolis into a world-class destination.

One of my chief concerns was having a safe place for my children while I was at work, so I enrolled them in a Catholic boarding school called Marie-Clarac, run by Italian nuns. The children would be there Sunday evening through Friday. A few weeks later, Josée decided to place her two boys in the same school, which made it a lot easier for all of us.

Josée and I agreed a move to a bigger apartment that our families could share made good sense. The two of us began searching and found a beautiful four-bedroom apartment in a modern building with a swimming pool on the roof. We split the rent and our responsibilities with the four children. On weekends, the kids would spend time with their dads. We were all set!

I was making a decent salary at La Crêpe Bretonne. However, the schedule was too rigid, and I decided to look for another job. At the same time, I also wanted to help Josée find a new place to work.

The coming of Expo 67 improved the job market. With so many anticipated visitors to Montreal, the restaurant business was booming, and I found a French restaurant, Au Pied de Cochon, that had an opening for a waitress. The owner was Georges and his French chef was a man named Charly Beaudry. The food was excellent, each plate coming out of the kitchen beautiful to behold.

I was unfamiliar with a lot of the plates on the restaurant's menu. My mother had taught us cooking, but her dishes were adapted to Spanish and Arab influences. They were nothing like the French gourmet offerings at Au Pied de Cochon. Charly soon realized I wasn't experienced with his kind of food as a waitress.

I needed the job badly and really wanted to learn. So I approached Charly and asked for help. He gladly gave me the proper training, and we became good friends.

When I recall that time, I recognize how important the experience was to me and my future: it introduced me to fine cooking. Years later, in 1976, I bought a restaurant in Montreal with Denise Vallier, a partner friend of mine. We named the restaurant La Marguerite and served French specialties and crêpes. So my restaurant experience in the 1960s helped me gain confidence to be successful in the future. For me, the "school of life" and working with the best has always paid great dividends.

As I mentioned earlier, Alain, my dear brother, decided to move to Canada. He arrived in the middle of April 1967, just a few days before the opening of Expo 67.

Alain didn't have good news about our father. He told me, "The day I was liberated from my military service, I was walking with a friend down Boulevard Saint-Michel in Paris. As I passed a newsstand, I saw our father's name in a headline about the disappearance of a rich woman. The story stated that the number-one witness had been interrogated."

He went on to tell me he made it to Mom's apartment and discovered several newspaper journalists waiting at her door. "They started asking me questions," he said, and I could tell the whole affair had greatly upset him.

Life became a nightmare for my mother as well as for the rest of the family. We found out Dad was accused of killing at least one wealthy elderly lady, perhaps more! Once again, the ugly history of my father reared its head.

I knew what my father was like; he'd been doing very bad things since my childhood. Father's new lady friend, Dee Dee, was his accomplice, and both of them would have to answer to the law.

Now, more than ever, I appreciated being in Canada far away from France. I wanted to shield my children from the nightmare of my dad. Of course, it was much harder on my sister and mother. In Paris, they had to hide their faces in shame. I felt safer thousands of miles away.

It finally seemed likely that Dad would be locked up for a long time, which was a shame, since he had everything needed for a successful life, being a good-looking, intelligent man. But he had the devil in his heart, and although he was charming with the ladies, he had no respect for human life. People like him were a torture to their family. A veritable monster!

24

Expo 67

It was time to get busy and help Alain find work. After all, life had to go on. Soon, he got a job as a busboy clearing tables of dirty dishes at Auberge de Saint-Tropez. It was good for him to be working. He had just turned twenty-one when he arrived in Montreal.

Our group of friends got bigger. Most of them were French, and we looked out for one another. Isn't that what life was about? We lived, we loved, we learned. We were all young, willing to work hard, ready for good things in our new environment.

Getting around Montreal wasn't always easy, even with public transportation. We had no car, and obviously, life would be a lot better with one. So I applied for a $1,000 loan and got it approved.

With the money I was making at the restaurant and the loan, Bruno and I were able to buy our first car—a used Plymouth Valiant. This American car was a real blessing for Josée and me. With it, I could pick up our four children each Friday afternoon at Marie-Clarac and return them on Sunday night or Monday morning.

As it turned out, Expo 67 was an incredible event that ran from April 27 to October 29. The theme was "Man and His World," and an amazing amount of work was completed for it in a very short time. Canadians had to really hustle to be ready for the fair's opening. One of the new marvels prepared for Expo was a subway. When it was launched in October 1966, Montreal's Metro was only Canada's second subway system, the first being in Toronto. But it was the very first in North America to run on rubber tires instead of metal wheels.

For six months, we earned a very good living feeding people from around the world who paid us well. It was a real-life *conte de fées* or fairy tale! Josée was able to get a waitress job and finally make a decent living serving tables. And as I mentioned before, Alain had a job and was earning his own money. It was possible that I worked more during this time than I ever had. Life then was full of energy and discovery, the way it should be. There was love, colors, music, food, and rides! Montreal was awesome and addictive, just like Paris.

On the opening day of Expo 67, visitors were treated to a gleaming futuristic spectacle. A monorail snaked through the immense grounds located on 900 acres of man-made and existing islands in the St. Lawrence River adjacent to Montreal. There was an oversized Buckminster Fuller geodesic dome, along with a very innovative housing complex known as Habitat 67.

The exposition was truly an international affair with universal appeal. Ninety pavilions represented Man and his World, including Indians of Canada, which was devoted to Indigenous art and culture and featured historical and political commentary concerning the past and present issues facing these people. The National Indian Council, the Indian Expo Task Force, and others were involved in the planning and creation of this pavilion, which stood separate from Canada's. I can't help but wonder if back then this was the beginning of raising the cultural awareness in Canada of what had been done to the Indigenous people of the country.

My brother had not only found a new country and job in Canada; he also met and fell in love with the woman who became his bride—Hélène Boisvert, a schoolteacher and native of Montreal. She was very artistic and shared her love of art in the way she decorated their eventual apartment.

Having a home and a woman he loved made Alain a happy man. I never heard them talk about having children, though, which surprised me. Wasn't that what we did when we fell in love and married? I suppose that was how I viewed it from my own experience. Perhaps Alain was scared to raise a child. Today, I'm happy he didn't. I now realize he didn't have the tools to be a parent. He was broken just like me and had suffered too much as a child.

Alain often spent time with Bruno Junior and Murielle. He spoiled them and taught them all he knew about hunting, sharing every detail, including cleaning and plucking feathers from geese and ducks, then cutting open their bellies to empty the guts. I learned how to cook these birds, like the French, making pâtés and sauces.

My sister-in-law wasn't into cooking or cleaning birds, but she offered to help with my children, which delighted me. The Marie-Clarac school was only a few minutes away from where she and Alain lived.

There was much that was new to me in Canada. I knew in my heart I needed to fight to find peace. Things were so hard with Bruno. He basically lived his life without me. However, his schedule did allow him to visit Expo and La Ronde, the nearby amusement park, after work during the week or on weekends.

I wasn't afraid to try new things. Sure, I worked long hours and dealt with the public, but I was a hard worker and willing to do whatever it took to get along. I relied on our growing group of friends, and having my brother close was reassuring. All of us who were immigrants found ways to help one another.

Expo 67 closed its doors after six months. It was a big success and attracted 50 million visitors to a country with a population of only 20 million at the time. In essence, the fair more than doubled the country's population and set a per-capita record for world exhibition attendance. Canada used the event to project an image of unity and put its best face forward to the international community. It was a transformative event for Montreal, and even after the city slowly returned to its normal pace, it was never the same as before.

25

Into the Wilderness

It wasn't just Montreal that wouldn't be the same after Expo 67. Our life was about to change in a major way. Bruno had decided he wanted a better job than working at the Citroën garage. One day, he told me he'd met a new friend who was employed at a mine in Thompson, Manitoba. The work there paid much more than what he could make in Montreal. When he told me he was going there alone, I was speechless!

What had been building for some time was finally happening, but maybe it was for the best. We both needed a break from each other.

Fortunately, before his departure, Bruno helped us move to a new apartment. Now that the Expo was over, rents had returned to their less-expensive prices, so there was no reason to share one big apartment. That meant Josée and her family also had to move. I was happy they were able to find a place within walking distance of our new apartment. Having her close helped me look at the bright side of life.

After Bruno left, I relied more and more on my group of friends. I needed assistance determining my options and how to handle the future. I really wanted to keep the children with me and not have to send them off to Marie-Clarac every Sunday night. It was agony to have them away the rest of the week. I missed them so much but had to work now more than ever.

Weeks passed with no communication from Bruno whatsoever. Maybe he'd just literally written me off!

Finally, with Christmas just a week away, a letter arrived telling me Bruno was coming to visit for a week. That very day I called Marie-Clarac and informed it that Bruno Junior and Murielle wouldn't be returning after the Christmas break. Then I quit my job and told my landlord we'd be leaving.

I was throwing caution to the wind, but I'd had enough. It was time to confront Bruno. I found it intolerable to keep my children away from me so much of the time. Perhaps I didn't have a plan, but I was doing what I felt was right.

When Bruno arrived at the apartment, I told him I refused to be left alone and continue having our children at a boarding school. He wasn't amused. In fact, he was furious!

I needed him to understand that I was at a breaking point. Working hard all week, I was emotionally and physically exhausted. The children needed to be with us, to be with their parents.

Bruno was happy to see the children after being away for several months. He decided we needed to stay together as a family and made arrangements for a place for all of us in Thompson.

We began preparations for the long drive—more than 1,800 miles across Canada—into a rugged northern landscape of pristine lakes, rapid rivers, rocky outcrops, wild animals, and primeval forests. Winters in Thompson meant months of cold and snow. The temperature could drop to forty degrees below zero for days. In such extreme winter weather, a person could easily get frostbite, so it was important to cover up as much skin as possible.

"Farewell, my dear friend. I'm going to miss you," I told Josée when we got together next. She cried, and so did I.

"You've been a very good friend to me, Janine, and I'm so glad we met and were able to share time together. You're a blessing to me."

What a dear! I thought. It was hard to say goodbye, but I felt reassured about my decision when Alain told me I was making the best choice for my kids.

Bruno was the driver, and he was a good one. The first day, we drove for ten hours. Fortunately, we made it without any problems, since the highway was pretty clear. Naturally, progress would be slower when it did snow. But during the occasional squall, Bruno learned to get behind big-wheel trucks, which seemed safer.

During the long drive, we didn't speak much. Bruno gave me the silent treatment, making me feel like an outcast. When he did talk to me, he accused me of infidelity, perhaps his attempt to cover up his insecurities. Making my life miserable made him feel better about himself.

I'd become accustomed to Bruno's jealousy, but it always turned me off. He constantly accused me of cheating on him, and my best policy was to remain quiet. One of the big frustrations on the trip to Thompson was how little he was concerned about us. I had to plead with him to stop for food, since he was driving and had all the money and control over when and where to spend it. All I cared about was what was best for my children. The trip was already a nightmare for us, but it was only the beginning!

Eventually, we made it to Winnipeg, the last big city before heading north into a wilderness that wasn't for the faint of heart. It was a world away from the bright lights of Montreal. Along the way, we spotted moose, black bears, wolves, and foxes.

I was grateful the children were comfortable and warm in the back seat of the car. Most of the time they slept. Surprisingly, the road from Winnipeg to Thompson was clean and plowed, a necessity for trucks moving heavy loads to and from the mines.

Driving through the day and night, Bruno did well behind the wheel, and finally, we glimpsed the lights of Thompson. I was excited, but Bruno continued not talking to me, perhaps too intent on driving.

Then, suddenly, around 11:00 p.m., Bruno pulled the car to the side of the road and announced we were out of gas. It was December 31, 1968, New Year's Eve, and we were all alone in the night with two small children. No more heat. Dangerously cold. What a way to end a year! There was nothing left to do but pray.

Getting out of the car to see how close we were to Thompson, I glimpsed it in the distance, still a long way off and certainly too far to walk. Bruno had misjudged how far we could go after the last fill-up, but I knew better than to accuse him of negligence. The thought came to me that we could freeze to death!

I turned around and looked behind us. What was that—a light in the distance? After what seemed like an eternity, the headlights of a big truck appeared. The driver stopped next to our car, filled our tank with gas, and left. No money was requested. Not a word exchanged. He simply performed the good deed and departed. An angel had come to our aid!

My heart swelled with gratitude as I wondered who had just helped us.

Perhaps an Indigenous spirit?

"You're like a cat," Bruno said. "If we threw you from a roof, you'd land on your paws."

He was right. This wasn't the first time I'd felt the mysterious and miraculous hand of the Divine. Nor would it be the last.

Situated along the Burntwood River, 473 miles north of Winnipeg, Thompson was the largest city in Manitoba's Northern Region. However, it might as well have been on another planet.

The so-called "Hub of the North" was home to caribou, moose, bears, beavers, and numerous species of birds. A perfect place for true adventurers in the warmer months, it was a magnet for those willing to explore a beautiful wilderness. During the winter, though, it was a different story and not easy to live there. Most of the residents worked in the mines, digging out nickel sulfide, copper, cobalt, gold, and silver.

A large Indigenous population has lived in the Thompson region for countless generations: Cree, Ojibway, Dakota, Dene, and others. Their cultural influences are still present from food to art and spiritual practices. However, the dark side of Western civilization has gravely affected these First Nations peoples.

When we finally arrived in Thompson, our first stop was in front of a motel with an attached restaurant. Bruno left us in the car while he checked us into the motel. When he returned, he escorted us into the restaurant. As the door was opened, I saw a bar full of people drinking and smoking cigarettes. There was loud music and chanting. It was the first time I'd seen Indigenous women drinking and mixing with white men. How sad that much of what was brought to these people from our so-called civilized lifestyles was negative.

We were greatly relieved to finally be off the road. Once we finished eating and bedded down in the motel, we didn't leave for several days. It was much too cold to take a chance. What we needed was warmer clothes. Without proper protection, a few minutes outside was enough to freeze limbs.

Eventually, we got the children outfitted. However, Bruno wasn't willing to buy me proper clothing. Once again, it was clear that I'd made a big mistake giving him my hard-earned money to keep for our trip. I badly needed my own cash.

After a few days, Bruno introduced me to a large French-Canadian family who had lived in Thompson for years. These simple but kind folks offered us the basement in their house to rent. I didn't mind at first, but soon the place was full of cigarette smoke and people drinking, not an ideal environment for our young children.

A few months later, one of Bruno's friends left Thompson, and we were able to move into a modern apartment. What a relief! It was perfect for our little family. The children started school and improved their English. I, too, enhanced my English, but mainly by watching television. One TV show in particular helped me. *Gilligan's Island* was a tale of seven people who set out on a three-hour sightseeing tour on the charter boat *Minnow*. They were caught in a storm, swept off course, and ended up stranded on a deserted tropical island.

The comedy had us laughing at their exploits as the diverse group of castaways kept trying to get off the island only to fail in some way. The children and I loved watching the show together, repeating the English words to one another.

I needed a job and found one at a food camp for the mines. A French-Canadian woman in her fifties ran the camp and put me in charge of making sandwiches for the workers. Each miner presented a list, and I prepared their sandwiches and fruit. It was an easy job and gave me some income for our family.

The miners were served over countertops, so I didn't have any direct contact with them. That didn't stop Bruno from being suspicious. Again, he stopped talking to me, except to tell me he didn't like the way the men looked at me or complimented me. It seemed as if he was unhappy with me all the time. Worse, Bruno kept me from having new friends, which was sheer torture.

He could also do some very humiliating and mean things. One time, we were invited to a party. I bought a bottle of Scotch to share, but before we left for the event, he poured it out on my head! I was all dressed and ready to greet our friends at the party, but now everything was ruined. After that, Bruno took off and stayed away for two days.

I didn't want to live this way anymore. At the time, I didn't know there was a name for the kind of person Bruno was. But now I know. Such a person is called a narcissist.

26

To British Columbia

After two years of living hell, I had to get away from Bruno. We were no longer a match, if we ever were; all we had in common were our children. I'd had enough of his coldness and enough of Thompson's frigid winters. Montreal had been frosty and could have pretty severe winters, but I couldn't handle the temperatures in Thompson that dropped far below zero for weeks on end. Just like a lion forced to live in Siberia, if I didn't get out of there, I'd die. Warmth and sunshine were what I craved.

So I came up with an escape plan that would still involve Bruno, at least for a while. I shared a magazine with him with pictures of British Columbia and Vancouver Island. We kept looking at the beautiful pictures and fell in love with the landscape. There was no snow, no ice, but instead luxurious forests and picturesque flowers, also gorgeous lakes, rapid rivers, and the sea. Bruno was clearly motivated to try something new. He was growing weary of the harsh living in Thompson, not to mention the brutal labor in the mines.

We took a trip to Winnipeg to shop for a new vehicle and bought a brand-new blue Volkswagen bus. Returning to Thompson, we quickly packed our belongings. I was so excited and wanted to leave this ice world before Bruno changed his mind.

I'd worked hard, just as much as he had, and contributed to our savings. But Bruno was the only bank account. He held the purse strings and controlled all our purchases. It was always such a big deal for him to spend money, even on necessities. He'd buy a bag of apples and just eat that. Where was his concern for us, his family? I was his wife in name only. Ironically, he continued to be ridiculously jealous and always suspicious of me but never demonstrated that he really cared about me.

The problem was that I didn't love him anymore. I needed to be without him and all the baggage he made me own, but I had to get out of Manitoba first, so I tried to stay positive with him.

Surprisingly, at that time, our relationship took a better turn. Bruno became more interested in my happiness, which was a welcome change, but I knew it wouldn't last. It was only a matter of time before he'd start harassing me again.

Bruno was good at making me feel guilty all the time. It depressed me to be around him. I couldn't really talk to him and certainly didn't trust him. I never gave him any reason to be jealous, but that didn't make a difference.

He was never physically violent with me and knew I wouldn't let him or anyone hurt me. If he ever tried to get physical with me, he realized I'd hurt him back. After all I had been through growing up, I'd learned to protect myself.

So we started planning our trip to British Columbia. Although Bruno could be secretive, I think he looked forward to the change. He needed to find his own peace, but I knew I was never going to be the one to change him.

FRENCH TWIST

Already in Canada we'd traveled through Quebec, Ontario, and Manitoba. Now we'd be crossing Saskatchewan and Alberta to reach Vancouver in British Columbia. By the time we reached Alberta, we were all in a good mood. The landscape changed dramatically, and there was much beauty on the drive. We visited Calgary and the remarkable resort town of Banff. The peaks of Mounts Rundle and Cascade, part of the Rocky Mountains, dominated Banff's skyline.

Our little blue bus was a good purchase and got great gas mileage. Everything we owned was in the Volkswagen, and our kids had room to sleep and be comfortable. We lived like migrants or, more romantically, like Roma.

Continuing westward, we found the landscape in British Columbia so unlike the rest of Canada. Known as the Cordillera Region, it included vast forests, enormous mountain ranges, deep valleys, and swift rivers. The climate on the Pacific coast was mild and wet, and the snow that fell rarely lingered. Inland it was drier with much more snow, but nothing like what we'd experienced in Thompson. We spent a few days in the Okanagan Valley, an area famous for fruit orchards and wineries, a place rich in grapes, apples, pears, peaches, apricots, cherries, and plums.

Our spirits were lifted. Even Bruno smiled more frequently. Several times he mentioned how miserable he'd been in Thompson's mines, places he said weren't even fit for animals.

27

Arrival on the West Coast

It was a relief to be away from the dire living conditions of the past couple of years in Manitoba. Each day our world looked better and better. Too bad that feeling didn't last.

Initially, Bruno didn't tell me what his plans were for a job in British Columbia. It turned out he decided to work in a mine again, this time for a company called Britannia, which had been extracting copper ore around Mount Sheer on the eastern shore of Howe Sound since 1903. He applied for a job, was hired, and started immediately.

The closest town to the mine was Squamish, a place with small-town charm and epic attractions to rival any major tourist destination. Located at the northern tip of Howe Sound, Squamish was surrounded by majestic mountains, most impressively the Stawamus Chief, an immense granite monolith. There was also the sea-to-sky gondola providing views of island-dotted Howe Sound. Nearby was Shannon Falls, a towering cascade.

It was an awesome spot to live. We found an apartment, furnished it with used furniture found locally, and registered our children for school. Life was good again.

Within a couple of months, however, Bruno's moody self resurfaced, his usual pattern, disrupting our lives and creating tension once more. He quit his job at the mine and found a new one in logging. Large forests were abundant in this part of the country, and maybe he wanted to work aboveground in nature. Or perhaps he merely desired a change of scenery or better wages. It was hard to know anything about Bruno. He did what he wanted and rarely, if ever, discussed anything with me.

I wasn't working yet, and soon life became horribly intolerable. Again, Bruno stopped talking to me, but this time I refused to put up with his behavior and asked him to leave. "I don't love you anymore," I told him. "I want out of this marriage!"

"Okay, then I'll go. No sense staying here. Besides, logging isn't for me."

He left us, disappearing for weeks. I met new people and decided to return to work the first chance I got. It didn't matter what, really, just as long as I could earn some income and provide for my children. So I approached the manager of our apartment building and asked for work. He gave me a job cleaning the seven buildings of the complex and the swimming pool. I worked at night while the children slept. The paycheck wasn't much, but it was enough for the kids and me to live on.

Eventually, Bruno came back. He'd changed his mind, saying he wanted to be with us. But I was done. All I needed was time to work out a plan. I was at a real turning point in my life and was determined not to be tied to a man I no longer loved or wished to be around.

In one of the apartments of the complex, I met a lady tenant with whom I struck up a friendship. Anne McLean was married to a long-distance truck driver named Sigurd who owned a truck and was on the road a lot driving across Canada from British Columbia to Quebec. She was alone most of the time, and we became friends. Anne was someone I could trust, something I really needed then.

We helped each other, and our children became fast friends. Together, we went to Vancouver Island to camp or fish. It was a wonderful time for our four children and us as we enjoyed the outdoors and gave one another moral support. Once again, I was blessed with a good friend.

There weren't a lot of opportunities for decent work in Squamish, so Anne and I decided to relocate farther south. We waited for Sigurd to return from one of his road trips and move us to apartments in Surrey, next door to the big city of Vancouver. A lovely area with affordable housing and many schools, our new home also possessed great services and activities for families.

It was an ideal place for immigrants. There was a large, diverse community that welcomed newcomers. Almost half of the residents spoke something other than English as their first language, which helped us settle in and feel accepted. For the first time in my life, I was truly free to do as I pleased.

Soon, I found a job at the Cave Supper Club in Vancouver, a renowned nightspot known for high-class entertainment. The Cave opened for business in 1937. By the time I was employed there in 1970, it was an iconic club where famous entertainers such as James Brown, Bette Midler, Ray Charles, Peggy Lee, Johnny Cash, Sonny and Cher, Liza Minnelli, and many others had performed.

I was a cocktail waitress and made a very good living. Just twenty-seven and free like an eagle, when I think of that time, I smile. It was perhaps the best time of my life.

With my new job, which I loved, I no longer paid attention to what Bruno felt about me. He was completely out of my heart, and I didn't want to see him anymore. I was now surrounded by great shows and wonderful music. What was more, I was making many new friends.

My thoughts often turned to the night in Manitoba when we'd been stranded on the road, out of gas, and in danger of freezing to death. Was it a miracle that out of nowhere a stranger in a truck arrived and filled our tank with gas? It was the first time I'd witnessed a miracle, something I'd never forget or ever get out of my mind.

While I'd never been formally religious, I knew something was speaking to me, to my soul. I found myself believing in God and the power of the Holy Spirit. Or the Spirit of the First Nations. Weren't they all connected?

I'd been baptized before I turned two in a Catholic church in Rabat. My godmother was Señora María, a loving soul from Portugal. When I was a child, she saw me every Christmas, and one year gave me a beautiful gold chain. Attached to the chain was a medal of the Blessed Mother of Jesus. I loved Señora María dearly, but she died before we left Morocco.

Over time, I suppose, I'd lost my childlike faith. Going to church had never really interested me that much, and religion was boring. But, later, my faith was restored in the kindness of people and the beauty of nature. I now see God in people and animals. Something tells me there's more to life than what we can see.

An experience working at the Cave reinforced that notion. My job required handling my customers' tabs. During the show, we had to get cash to make change for large bills. One day at the club, I was getting into my work clothes when I overheard one of the waitresses mention that our cashier was missing $50 and was forced to pay for her mistake. All of us sympathized with her loss. Then a thought came to me. I recalled that I had more money left from my tips. I didn't say anything right away, but it occurred to me that the money missing from the cashier's drawer must have been my tip earnings from the day before.

I thought about giving myself excuses, but I felt sick to my stomach, so I chose to go to the cashier and give her the $50. She was very surprised and thanked me.

Later, my boss walked over to my section during the show. The lights were down, and it was dark. "Janine, when you get a break, can you come to my office?"

"I'll be right there," I replied. Of course, I was nervous.

When I entered the office, he said, "Please sit down."

I did as he asked.

He smiled warmly. "I've owned the Cave for years, and no one's ever returned money. I own several businesses in town, and you'll always have a job."

That was my second miracle!

During this time, I had two jobs. The first was in the day waitressing in a restaurant from 10:00 a.m. until 3:00 p.m. It was owned by the proprietor of the Cave, and I've long since forgotten its name, but it provided a helpful second income. My hours at the Cave were from 5:00 p.m. until midnight. When the club's show was a hit, we sold lots of drinks, and the tips were great. It wasn't easy working so much and certainly not an ideal situation, but I had to pay the bills. Gratefully, Anne McLean babysat my children after school and fed them.

It would have been nice to get help from Bruno, but he'd moved to Alaska. He never told me why, except that the wages were much higher than those in British Columbia.

Bruno returned months later. He called and told me he wanted to visit. Reluctantly, I agreed. When he arrived, I opened my door, just as I had for many years and continued to do for a few more. All I wanted was to keep my children happy. They'd been through enough and did love their father. So I went along with his visits to my home. At times, Bruno spent a week, at others longer. But once he started questioning my private life, I stopped him and told him to leave.

He revealed nothing about what was going on in his life, but one time he brought a male friend. They seemed pretty close, and I wondered if he was gay and in a relationship with my husband. I asked him, but he denied it, telling me it was all in my head.

Bruno disclosed that he and his friend had made plans to drive south until they reached the Panama Canal where they'd board a ship to Australia. It sounded like another of Bruno's crazy schemes.

It really upset me when he told me all I had to do while he was away was to sign his monthly unemployment card in his name and cash his check. That made me crazy! I refused to stay by myself in British Columbia and be a part of his illegal plan.

28

Back to Quebec

It was 1972, and after all that had happened, I was convinced I had to return to Montreal to be close to my only family in Canada—Alain and Hélène. When I called Alain, he told me, "Come back. We want you closer." It was important to have my brother's support.

Bruno stayed in British Columbia with his friend. He bought three airline tickets and drove us to the airport, destination Montreal. Then he sold the Volkswagen bus and our furniture but refused to send me a check for my part of the sales. That was no surprise, though! In my heart, he was already in the past. It was time to move on.

Leaving the beauty of British Columbia and returning to the cold, harsh winters of Quebec was difficult, but I knew it was the right thing to do. I had to get away from Bruno and be with people who supported me and my decisions.

The children and I left behind good memories when we flew to Montreal. I promised to enroll them in an English-speaking school. By now they were bilingual and able to speak both French and English.

However, I realized it would spark an unfavorable reaction from Alain and Hélène to put them in an English school. My brother's wife was a French-Canadian teacher and couldn't accept my doing such a thing. To her it was a sin. Keeping French alive and well in Quebec was very important to her. But to me it wasn't a problem. I spoke three languages—French, English, and Spanish—and dabbled in a few more such as Italian, Arabic, Portuguese, and Greek. I wanted my children to appreciate the diversity of different languages.

Bruno Junior and Murielle were eager to return to Montreal where they could visit with Alain and Hélène again. For his part, my brother would be happy to see them. They'd grown into sweet children with whom he'd always enjoyed spending time.

As for me, I looked forward to renewing my friendship with Josée. Going through some changes of her own, she'd separated from her husband and was enjoying being free and independent, something I, too, craved. I had no idea what to do next beyond taking care of my children and getting a divorce. The latter would happen, but not for a while. No longer with her husband, Josée had progressed in her work life. She now managed a French restaurant in Old Montreal.

Our reunion was a joy! Josée welcomed me with open arms.

"I'm so happy to see you, my dear friend!" she cried.

"How are you, Josée?" I asked.

"Fantastic! I'm so happy now—even more so to see you!"

It was so wonderful to see she was doing so well. And she hadn't lost her touch for hospitality. She prepared a delicious meal for us—quail flambé au cognac, a French specialty.

Afterward, she told me, "Please stay here tonight. We'll have more time to catch up."

Later, she helped me find an apartment where we had English-speaking neighbors and were close to the children's school. Plus, her financial assistance helped us get settled. What an angel! Josée also introduced me to a new French restaurant, La Lucarne, owned by a French-Canadian couple. They quickly hired me. In fact, I was back working the very same day.

It amazed me how in only a few years life had changed for all our friends. Quebec's economy was doing poorly, but I was fortunate to find a job. More importantly, I had support from family and friends.

The French chef from Au Pied de Cochon, Charly Beaudry, had become a partner in a new restaurant called Chez Georges. I was happy to learn he'd married his high school sweetheart and were expecting their first child. They were neighbors and friends with Alain and Hélène and often spent their free time together. It was so nice to be part of a cheerful, upbeat group. Charly's wife was Annie, a real peach, always smiling, kind, and full of energy.

Once we became settled again in Montreal, I had a desire to return to Paris to visit my mother. I wanted her to see my children again. Also, I was curious about what had become of my father. So I planned the trip for the summer while the children were on vacation from school.

29

Visit to Paris

Mom didn't tell me much about my father when she wrote us. I think she was trying to protect us from bad news, but it was agony not to know what had really happened to Dad.

When we arrived in Paris, I rented a car. My first goal was to visit my sister, France. She'd been living with Mom in Paris but had moved after marrying a Frenchman she'd met in a Mormon church. They lived in a small village in the southwest of France, ten hours from Paris.

I loaded the car with the family and started the long drive south. It was a full car with Mom; her companion, Yves; my little brother, Richard; and my two kids. I had to hear for myself what my sister was planning to do with the funds our grandmother had transferred to her before our father's trial. As far as I was concerned, at least half that money belonged to Mom. All his life, Dad forged her signature and used her name to hide his illegal activities.

When we got to France's place, confronting her was a disappointment.

She didn't react well at all and became aggressive, breaking my heart. France no longer seemed like my sister, certainly not the same one before I moved to Canada. Everyone knew the money was dirty. Mom, though, asked me to stop talking about it with France, insisting she didn't want it. Like the good mother she was, she wanted to preserve peace in our family. So I decided to drive away with the kids and Mom, continue south, and get to a beach in Spain. Whenever things heated up, I always took off.

The trip gave me time to cool off and talk about Dad with Mom. As I drove, I listened as she told me about him and the trial. "I begged the judge to spare his life."

"Why? He didn't deserve it."

"I did it for the sake of you, France, and Alain. It would have been too traumatic for all of you otherwise."

See how she was? Always thinking of what was best for us. But I didn't see it her way. I needed more time to process, to heal. However, our time in Spain relaxing on the beach was good for our morale.

Food and music also worked miracles. They helped me forget the painful reality. And being back in Spain where Mom was born was good for her, too.

We drove back to France to my sister's home, but I didn't talk further about the cash she was hiding.

Before leaving Paris, Mom had handed me a letter Dad had written to me. She had waited until the last day to give it to me. Once again, she was thinking of me and how the letter would affect me. She was so perceptive and knew it might upset me.

The letter was written from jail. In it, Dad said he was upset that I hadn't told him I'd moved to Canada. Basically, he was asking for his money and wanted France's address. I cut the letter into pieces and threw it in the trash.

30

Return to Montreal

It was 1972, and I was intent on putting the past behind me. I picked up another job renting and selling televisions. Martin Lubbert, my new boss, was a client from Lucarne. We struck up a friendship, and he convinced me I could work in the evenings and earn good commissions selling TV sets. I was good at it and began to make more money than I did waitressing.

Martin owned an electronics store and hired me to meet potential customers. I went to their homes to explain the benefits of renting or buying a television and get them to sign an agreement. Eventually, I started working full-time for Martin selling all types of electronics, not just televisions but also stereos and microwaves. It took some time, but life got easier.

Not just happy with my selling abilities, Martin also wanted an intimate relationship with me and never left me alone. He had a good heart and was great around Bruno Junior and Murielle, but I wasn't ready for something more with Martin.

An active man and a hard worker, he came from Holland and spoke

English with a Dutch accent. I considered him my teacher and a friend, someone I enjoyed being around. However, there were times when he could be authoritarian, something I didn't like.

Martin wanted me to love him, but I'd learned from my years with Bruno how necessary it was to have balance in a relationship. Intuitively, I knew we didn't have that, not enough for him to be a good companion. We did have fun, though. Our favorite pastime was riding horses. I'd never been around a farm, so the visits to Martin's horse farm were wonderful.

And then life once again threw me for a loop.

31

The Accident

It was a Saturday, and I went to the store early to get a list of potential customers to call and perhaps interest in renting a television set. Most of our customers were immigrants with whom I could connect. Martin advertised a $19-per-month rental, but I convinced clients to buy a TV when I told them they could get a brand-new unit for the same price and own it after thirty-six months.

On this particular day, I drove to the store with my little dog. After parking, I locked the dog in the car and started across the street when, suddenly, another car hurtled very fast toward me! I tried to get out of the way, backing up between parked cars, but the driver hit the front of my car and pushed it into another vehicle, sandwiching my knees between them.

I glanced up at the car that hit me and saw all four doors open simultaneously. The occupants jumped out and ran away, leaving the scene. Later, the police discovered the car was a rental. The driver had fled so quickly that he'd left the rental papers in the glovebox, which helped the police to find and arrest him.

The pain from the accident was almost unbearable, rendering me unable to walk, the muscle above my right knee severed. The police were called, and I was taken to a hospital.

Martin was phoned, and when he saw me in the hospital, he began to cry. I must have seemed pretty bad. My recovery was a long process, so Martin moved into my apartment to take care of me and also the children.

It was good to have Martin there, since it was so hard for me to get around. My legs were very swollen and blue, and just getting to the bathroom was difficult. As an independent person, that frustrated me a great deal. However, sometimes a person had to accept help when circumstances required. I was grateful for Martin's assistance. He was a kind and fun person whom I enjoyed being around, but I just wasn't ready for a serious commitment.

As I healed, I started to feel much better. During this time, I realized I wasn't the kind of woman to be locked up in Martin's world. My convalescence had given me plenty of time to think about that. I'd already been in a grueling relationship with Bruno, so I wasn't going to submit to another man's requests that often seemed more like demands. As such, I made a decision—time to get another job!

My solution was to acquire a real-estate license, which would give me a good excuse to distance myself from Martin. After all, selling real estate required a lot of time and working non-traditional hours.

I passed the real-estate test and got my license, then walked away from Martin. Of course, it broke his heart, and I was sad about that. He was a good man, loved my children, and gave a good deal of his time to visit them. But I just wasn't the woman for him, especially since I wasn't in love with him. Even now it's hard for me to talk about Martin. I know I hurt him and didn't like to do that to anyone. Years later, I visited Martin in Holland and had a chance to make amends.

In 1974, I finally got a divorce from Bruno. He never came to court and didn't contest the case. In the end, he was ordered to pay me child support of $200 per month.

Bruno had never followed up on his scheme to move to Australia with his friend. Instead, he stayed in Canada and also worked in Alaska. With Bruno, I never knew what would happen next.

Even after the divorce, he often came to Montreal to spend time with our children. Perhaps it was foolish to let him stay in my home while he was there, but I tried to keep a sense of peace with our family. However, it really frustrated me the way he questioned the children, creating confusion about who the actual parent was. As far as I was concerned, that was me. I was the one with full-time custody and the day-to-day responsibilities. Bruno always undermined me, giving the children permission to do whatever they pleased. They were teenagers who certainly enjoyed being indulged by a father whose behavior created a lot of division.

32

Joy Owning a Restaurant

It was very hard work to own a restaurant, with long hours and lots of challenges. But it could also be quite rewarding. Alain and three of his friends found a restaurant for sale in Old Montreal called Maison de Beaujeux. They bought it and made it a fun place to visit with great entertainment and delicious French food.

By that time, I'd worked at a few different restaurants and had learned a thing or two about the business. Preparing and enjoying good food had been a passion of mine for a long time, one that had been developed more fully during my time in Canada.

Not long after Alain and his partners purchased Beaujeux, I found a little Italian restaurant for sale in a great location. With help from some associates, I bought it, but since we wanted to sell crêpes and other French cuisine, we changed the name and menu. La Marguerite soon became my new pursuit and love.

Denise Vallier was a longtime waitress friend from the staff I worked with at La Crêpe Bretonne. She was a very efficient waitress and became my partner in the purchase. We didn't have all the funding we needed, so we approached and got financing from Charly Beaudry, who helped us with the deposit. Sometimes assistance comes in surprising ways.

We opened with a terrace featuring six bistro tables and umbrellas, and soon the restaurant became a magnet for young and old alike. Some customers were from previous days who became fans of our establishment. It was a lot of work, but we had a good thing going.

I'd hoped my two children would help in the restaurant, but they refused, and I couldn't force them. Teenagers in any circumstances could be challenging, but especially when one of the parents, like Bruno, gave them cash all the time for their expenses. Not surprisingly, Bruno Junior and Murielle didn't want to wash dishes for me.

33

South for the Winter

It was Christmas 1976 in Montreal. Having grown very weary of the cold, I longed for a getaway to somewhere warmer. Alain was planning to fly to Acapulco, Mexico, with his wife and said, "Use my car and drive to Florida." That appealed to me. "Take the children," he added. "It'll be good for all of you. And bring Jean-Pierre for safety." He was one of Alain's employees.

Montreal was covered with snow and very cold when we started our journey. Since Jean-Pierre didn't have a license, I had to do all the driving, but I was nervous because I didn't have any experience doing so in a snowstorm should we hit one along the way. My kids and Jean-Pierre encouraged me, however, and I drove all the way to New York City, checked into a motel, and rested for the night.

As we left the cold and winter behind, my nomad heart awakened. I could sense it calling me to the sun, warmth, and ocean.

It was a great relief when we finally finished our long drive south that ended in the Florida Keys. We found a motel owned by an elderly woman and settled in, all of us excited to have arrived at our destination.

Unfortunately, Jean-Pierre generated some unwelcome turmoil. He bought liquor and gave it to my teenage kids. How stupid of him!

Murielle got very drunk and needed help. I was sleeping and woke up to this nightmare. Panicking, I started asking questions, beginning with Jean-Pierre. "How could you do something so dangerous? Don't you know how wrong this is?"

Jean-Pierre blinked owlishly at me. "I... I'm so sorry, Janine."

Returning to Montreal after the vacation wasn't fun for the fellow. I made his life hell! It made me angry every time I glanced in the rearview mirror and saw his face.

"You're so stupid!" I kept telling him over and over.

Back in Montreal, despite the cold, I found warmth in a big circle of friends. Most of them were French Canadians, but some were originally from France. We knew one another very well and felt extremely comfortable in such a reassuring community. However, political unrest in Quebec was dramatically transforming its society.

34

The Quiet Revolution

Enormous changes began to happen in Quebec in June 1960 when the province's Liberal Party came to power. It was led by Premier Jean Lesage, who launched several legislative initiatives aimed at reforming the corruption that had become so widespread in previous years. Transforming and improving the social and educational infrastructure was something long needed in Quebec. The influence of the Roman Catholic Church was removed from most secular activities, and government became more directly involved in economic development.

The province's privately owned power companies were consolidated into one government-owned entity, and a new provincial pension plan was established, creating a large pool of investment capital. A great deal was done during this period of Liberal Party activism, which became known as "The Quiet Revolution."

Federally, a dynamic new leader of the Liberal Party, Pierre Elliott Trudeau, was elected prime minister in 1968. He had strong ideas and inserted his personal influence into every aspect of Canadian society. Some people believed he was arrogant and autocratic, but his influence dominated the political history of the country from the late 1960s to the early 1980s.

Trudeau was mainly concerned with keeping Canada unified and maintaining good relations between English and French Canadians. Those, too, were the specialties of Quebec's Liberal Party and its new leader, Robert Bourassa, who swept into office as premier in 1970.

An intensified air of conflict had arisen in Quebec, and I wanted no part of it. Separatists were pushing for the province to break away from Canada and become an independent nation. There was the horrifying event known as the October Crisis in 1970 when terrorists from the Front de libération du Québec (FLQ) kidnapped British trade commissioner James Cross in Montreal. A few days later, they snatched and eventually murdered Pierre Laporte, Quebec's deputy premier, minister of immigration, and minister of labour.

Naturally, this situation alarmed big companies, which started moving out of Quebec, including Sun Life, which I bought life insurance from for myself. Since we were so far away from France, I wanted to make sure that if something happened to me, my kids would have something.

The salesman was Dieter Jasper, who introduced me to his boss, who, in turn, offered me a job as a life insurance agent. After a couple of weeks of training, I started knocking on doors for the company and did quite well, eventually even receiving a Woman Salesperson of the Month Award. When Sun Life relocated its head office to Toronto, I had to quit. It was a good job, and I'd done well at it, but the politics between French and English Canadians in Quebec ended that opportunity, since I had no interest in moving to Toronto. Fortunately, the chance to purchase the restaurant that became La Marguerite came about, so I switched my focus to that enterprise.

I was very busy at this time in my life. There was a lot of stress working long hours at La Marguerite and dealing with home life and two teenagers. Without notice, their father appeared in Montreal sporadically and unpredictably. Bruno would stay a few weeks, then suddenly announce he was leaving again, which was always hard on the children.

Also, I was sick during much of the winter. I never did get used to the cold and found myself with a persistent cough that lasted weeks on end. Cold urticaria was a condition caused by exposure to frigid temperatures. When I visited my doctor in September 1978, I'd been ill for days and was diagnosed with the disease. The doctor also told me I had a problem with one of my ovaries and needed surgery. All of this stoked more stress in my life.

And then I got a call from the police department, informing me that my sixteen-year-old daughter had been arrested at a rock concert. She'd been drinking and got into an altercation with the police officer who arrested her, biting his hand!

35

A New Direction

I called my brother, and he joined me at La Marguerite to sort things out concerning Murielle. I really needed time to figure out how I was going to get her out of the mess with the police as well as go forward with my life. The next day, I phoned Bruno and asked him to come and help me. There came a time when I realized I couldn't handle everything by myself, and this was one of those occasions.

Bruno was working as a diesel mechanic in Saudi Arabia, making very good money, so he needed time to get organized before returning to Canada. Up until now, he'd opposed every decision of mine when it came to the children. Now we had to work together for their benefit. For far too long, I'd been his milk cow. He'd learned to manipulate me through our kids. As I mentioned before, Bruno was generous with them and let them do anything they desired. Naturally, that undermined my efforts when it came to parenting.

So I decided to hand over the running of my home to Bruno. He'd visited us in Montreal numerous times and was familiar with our home. I figured it would be best for the children if he lived in the same location as they did. Continuity was very important.

All my life I'd compromised with Bruno as long as that benefited the children. Now it was time to give my ex-husband the chance to be the father he should have been all along. He never had a home to welcome them to, so I'd opened mine to him when he visited. Now I was handing it over to him so he could be the parent in charge.

Frankly, I needed a break. Bruno could move into my rental house, be there with and for the children, and I could get the break I sorely needed, which was vital to maintain my sanity. I didn't tell Bruno how long I'd be away. Truth was I didn't really have a plan.

Bruno Junior was now seventeen, Murielle sixteen. It wasn't easy being a single-parent mother. It was hard to face the truth of my situation; I felt like a failure and defeated.

The cold, the lack of sun, the frustrations of life's events, all motivated me to get away. I wanted to return to the Florida Keys, to the warm sun and beauty of the ocean.

Because I was co-owner of La Marguerite with Denise Vallier, I had to talk to her about my plans. I'd come to confide in her and found her encouragement concerning what I was planning helpful. She mentioned that her husband was interested in buying my shares in the restaurant. The economy at that time in Quebec wasn't great, so it was good to know I had someone I could sell to I could trust.

I kept the lease on my car and prepared for my vacation. It was going to be a long drive. Two of my closest employees were waiters Alain Menard and Jean-Paul Benejams. They were both in their twenties and excited to leave the cold and snow of Canada for a warm Florida vacation. Jean-Paul couldn't go right away but hoped to come down around Easter. However, I was thrilled that Alain asked if he could ride with me for the lengthy drive to Florida.

My friends gathered for a goodbye party at La Marguerite. I was a bit sad to leave because I'd grown close to so many of them. Some promised to visit me in Florida on their vacations.

Montreal was covered in snow and so cold that I decided to leave before the next snowstorm. I was off on yet another adventure. This time, though, it would perhaps be the greatest turning point in my life.

PART FIVE
United States

36

Living in the United States

My vision of someday living in the United States, the "Land of the Free," came true many years after I first envisioned it while sitting on a Moroccan beach with Carol, my American friend. Back then I was just an idealistic teenager. Now I was an independent woman, fiercely determined to live my life free from the stress, anxiety, and troubles of the past. My childhood friend had planted the seed of someday going to America. Now that dream was becoming a reality. However, I hadn't figured it all out yet. When I said goodbye to my family, they thought I was just going to spend some time away in Florida. As far as they were concerned, I was heading to a warmer climate where I could relax and improve my health.

It was 1979, and I was in my mid-thirties, burned out, and badly needing to regroup, not only for my physical health but mental, emotional, and spiritual, as well. Looking back, I see this was a pattern in my life—a new beginning every eight years.

Denise, my partner at the restaurant, organized a farewell party before

I departed. She invited about a dozen friends to celebrate my leaving. One of the waiters, Alain Menard, was willing to go with me to Florida and offered to pay half the gas for the trip. He was young, early twenties, a very shy and private person. But he was responsible, and I trusted him. Plus, I was happy to have company for the long drive.

I packed a large suitcase and another bag and put them in my car. There was one year remaining on my car lease. After that, I'd have to decide to either buy or return it. I'd managed to save $2,000 and was looking forward to payment for my shares of the La Marguerite restaurant. By no means was I rich, but it was enough for a new start.

Another snowstorm was heading our way. We had to get on the road, so we decided to leave the next morning. I went home and slept in my bed for the last time.

Before Alain and I left, Bruno Senior moved in for a couple of days. He agreed to stay and was trying to get a handle on running the house. Bruno soon discovered how challenging that was with two teenage children.

My ex-husband never really had a home for us. He was too busy living a life away, working in several different places, from Canada to Saudi Arabia, and even France where he essentially lived a bachelor's life while residing with his parents. The time he spent with our kids was mostly when he had them for the two months of summer vacation.

Very early in the morning, before getting on the road, I said my goodbyes to the children. Bruno Junior came to me, gave me a big hug, and wished me *bon voyage*. My son! I'd never forget the way he gazed at me. He was eighteen years old, his sister, Murielle, seventeen, but I felt as if I was leaving my babies. It made me sad. I was their age when I had them!

It was time to take a thorough appraisal of myself. I knew that was something I had to do. I couldn't keep doing things the same way. It was time to get in touch with my inner self, which meant being apart. Despite the problems I'd always had with Bruno, I still felt the children were in good enough hands with him.

Murielle was happy. She was Daddy's girl! Her father was her favorite. To his credit, he was always affectionate with both kids.

Leaving was bittersweet. I told them I'd do my best to be back soon, and though I didn't have a phone, I promised to stay in touch daily.

Perhaps it seemed as if I was fleeing from my children, but that wasn't it. I was running away from the intolerable cold. In my heart, there were two things I desired: to leave the harsh cold of Canada and to be an American. The latter had always been a dream, born on a beach in Morocco many years ago.

My Canadian friends—Ginette, Danielle, and Yolanda—didn't understand. Oh, how I loved those ladies! I had tried to tell them I wasn't feeling well, that Florida was where I could get some warm sunshine and cure what ailed me. Hopefully, they understood that.

Had I made mistakes? Certainly. Who didn't? By this time, though, that didn't stop me from leaving. I'd made up my mind and knew in my heart it was the right decision.

37

The Florida Keys

Adventures were always full of surprises and discoveries. I'd experienced that all my life. This time the sea was calling me: gentle waves, a bright and sunny sky, the tang of saltwater. I fell in love with the Florida Keys!

To anyone who really knew me, that wouldn't be a surprise. A million reasons come to mind why such a beautiful location and climate strongly appealed to me. I needed to reconnect with the scent of the ocean. The beauty of it filled a big space in my heart. It just felt right and so amazing.

All of this brought back many childhood memories. Born and raised on the shore of the Atlantic Ocean in Rabat, Morocco, I'd spent the first fifteen years of my life fishing and diving for seashells. Perhaps unconsciously, what I felt about Florida was a longing for something I badly missed.

Montreal to the Florida Keys was a long drive. The day Alain and I left, I picked him up at 6:00 a.m., anxious to get on the road. Alain shared an apartment with Paul Benejams, our restaurant chef. Short and slim, Alain was twenty-four and still inexperienced in many ways. He'd never been to the United States. I was older at thirty-six and vastly more experienced thanks to my many challenging life events. That wasn't saying I was better than him. It was just the facts.

Alain also didn't have a driver's license, so all the driving was up to me. But that wasn't a problem—I loved to drive. I'd done it once before when I'd brought my children with me on vacation to Florida.

My road companion was super-excited to be going with me all the way to Key West. He was a good copilot and read the maps and indicated the way to go. A French native who spoke no English, he was certainly a curious person and asked me a thousand questions.

"Why do you like the US?" he asked.

"I don't *like* the USA," I replied. "I love it!"

There was so much about the United States that I found interesting and enjoyable, so I decided to elaborate. "I love everything about the country." I smiled. "Everything except the food."

That first day we drove for eight hours. It had been especially cold and miserable, with snow falling, when we left Montreal, so I was eager to reach the US/Canada border and get farther south. When we entered the United States, we used our French passports to obtain six-month tourist visas.

I hadn't been following the news, but at that time there was a lot of tension between Cuba and the United States. A wave of Cuban refugees had fled Fidel Castro and his dictatorship, searching for a better life in America. They kept entering illegally, arriving in the Florida Keys aboard fishing boats. From there, many proceeded to Miami. They could be seen on the sides of roads as they emerged from hiding in the mangroves and begged for rides. Many were children. It was heartbreaking!

Eventually, Castro's regime decided to let all Cubans who wished to immigrate to the United States to board boats at the port of Mariel, west of Havana. In April 1980, thousands left Cuba. Cuban exiles in the United States rushed to hire boats to pick up relatives at the ports. Many US boat captains saw this as a financial opportunity and took advantage by charging thousands of dollars to make the trips. Over several months, 125,000 refugees came to Florida that way.

It was later discovered that Castro had forced prison inmates and mental hospital patients to join the flotilla, creating a lot of problems for the United States. Many of these refugees were classified as serious or violent criminals and were denied US citizenship.

Political unrest, as I mentioned before, affected me profoundly. It seemed wherever I lived instability occurred—fighting and civil wars, violence and suffering. This time, however, I had no fear, probably due to a combination of experience and being in what I considered the safest country in the world. I didn't let things depress me as much. Instead, I focused on my own adventure as an immigrant.

Alain and I finally reached Key Largo and marveled at the Florida beauty. I surveyed my surroundings and believed I was in paradise!

38

On the Ocean

Living by the ocean had a special appeal for me. But I could go further and live *on* the ocean. I'd never done such a thing, but one of my Canadian friends had given me the address and phone number for a houseboat rental in Tavernier on Key Largo. The owner was Ron Wood.

I called Ron to find out the details and prices for renting a houseboat. He invited us to stop on our way to Key West. His property was right on the beach. We pulled up and immediately noticed several pontoons and a dozen houseboats tied up and ready to rent. Ron greeted us and invited us to stay for lunch. We agreed, both of us very excited about the prospect of living on the ocean.

Alain and I sat under a tiki in the shade and enjoyed Ron's hospitality. He told us, "I came up from Chicago on a vacation with my wife and loved the lifestyle so much that I bought the property for future vacations. Soon after, I purchased my first houseboat and rented it to tourists. That was the start of a profitable business."

The idea of time on the ocean, spending lazy days on a houseboat, sounded idyllic. Alain and I reserved a rental for the next weekend, then departed Key Largo for Key West.

During the two-hour drive, I experienced an immediate relationship with the environment. Sunlight sparkled off pristine water, it was warm, and it felt right!

Key West was home to the world's third-largest living coral reef and was a vibrant ecosystem and subtropical paradise of natural beauty and romantic appeal. The place was also full of history.

Over the years, a wide variety of residents had lived in Key West: Indigenous people, Spanish and then British colonists, cigar makers, and "wreckers"—salvagers of old shipwrecks. A number of famous writers and bohemians had also made the Keys their home. Both Tennessee Williams and Ernest Hemingway had lived there for a time. Hemingway worked in the early-morning hours and whiled away the afternoons and evenings at local bars such as Sloppy Joe's, still a popular tourist hangout.

I wasn't famous, nor was I seeking celebrities. I just wanted a better life, one that was more fulfilling. Little did I know how many amazing changes and life experiences would happen in the years ahead.

After two days in Key West, Alain and I returned to Key Largo and rented the houseboat we'd reserved for the weekend. We weren't experienced boat people, but Ron was a very good teacher. He showed us how to maneuver our watercraft, and off we went to soak in the water life. We loved our new life so much that we called our friends in Montreal. They were stuck in the cold and snow, so we invited them to come down.

"Get out of the cold!" I told them on the phone. "It's incredible here."

Soon, Jean-Paul, one of Alain's friends, flew down to be with us. He was the other waiter at La Marguerite. There was enough room on the houseboat for the three of us. At night we docked at Ron's marina, while in the daytime we journeyed around the open water, fishing and diving for lobster. This was what I'd needed: an escape from Montreal's winters and enjoying warm, relaxing days. My life had completely changed for the better.

The change appealed to Alain, too. After a couple of weeks, Jean-Paul returned to Montreal. But Alain wasn't ready to fly back home and started cleaning houseboats for Ron, allowing him to trade labor for the rental of our own.

Alain, Ron, and I began hanging out. Ron and his wife had no children. She had moved back to Chicago, which had upset him greatly, so drinking and partying had become his chief pastimes. In the daytime, he took us out in his speedboat; in the evenings, we hopped from tiki bar to tiki bar. I wasn't much of a drinker but joined the fun, even sharing marijuana with the two men. I had to admit the cannabis helped me relax.

Although not overly religious at the time, I did believe in a spiritual world and miracles. My life experiences had confirmed the latter happened. So I started questioning my direction in life. Without Bruno Junior and Murielle, I seemed to lack purpose.

I didn't have a plan, but I knew returning to Montreal wasn't what I wanted. I craved freedom and desired a life with meaning. So what was my best option? I could go back to Paris and live with my mother. At least the weather there was better than Montreal's.

At the end of the school year, the children came to visit for a couple of weeks. They brought Tina, our dog. I had left her with them in Montreal. Oh, but I missed her! From that day on, Tina lived with me for ten more years—a constant and loving companion.

Being in Florida without US citizenship was risky, especially at that time. Immigration authorities and police were on constant alert, mainly due to the constant arrival of Cubans in Florida.

Every day I read the newspapers, searching for opportunities, for some way to earn income. One day, I found an interesting ad—a family looking for a nanny for their three children. I dialed their number and made an appointment to meet them.

The father was a heavyset man, probably in his fifties. He owned an accounting office. His wife had passed away, leaving him to parent his two girls and one boy. The kids were fourteen, twelve, and five. What a big challenge! Of course, I knew something about "single parenting." Essentially, I'd been doing that myself, since Bruno was mostly not around to share in those responsibilities.

The family lived in Homestead, about thirty-one miles away and basically a Miami suburb. I took the job and enjoyed taking care of the children, but I was lonely and needed a love of my own. I was also scared, afraid that as an illegal alien I'd be caught and deported. Breaking the law, hiding like a thief, in constant fear of being sent back to Canada were all just really hard. I dreaded the possibility of being sent back to the land of long and cold winters.

As so often in my life, I met a stranger who changed things for me. The accountant whose children I was watching during the day always had young women working for him. Most were in their twenties, and some stayed at the house with me and the kids.

One of these women was Marsha, tall with long legs and a beautiful smile. She was probably twenty-two or twenty-three at the time, was very knowledgeable about nutrition, and didn't eat meat. And she was a member of the Unification Church, a religious group considered by some people to be a cult. Its founder was Sun Myung Moon whose followers were often referred to as Moonies. The religion was a mix of Christianity and Buddhism; Moon was considered its Messiah, sent to complete the works of Jesus. Whatever one might think of the Moonies, I found Marsha to be a kind person.

Marsha spent a lot of time in closeted meditation. She was a quiet person but did open up to me and taught me about colonics, nutrition, and relaxation.

I was working as a nanny on the weekdays and had the weekends off. One time, I invited Marsha to come to Key Largo to meet Alain. I'd told her about him, and she was excited to see him.

From the moment they encountered each other, they were inseparable. Perhaps I possessed matchmaking skills I didn't know I had. Funny how life worked out.

My life thus far had often been a series of coincidences, and here was another example. There was a gas station and convenience store I frequently stopped at. The store was full of gadgets and souvenirs that I enjoyed browsing.

The manager was a gentleman about forty-five years old with curly gray hair and a charming smile. I loved the sound of his voice. We struck up a conversation, and I learned he was taking care of the store for a couple on a cruise around the world.

We ate lunch often and talked about our lives. His name was Darrell Eugene Carpenter. He was divorced and had worked in the hair industry, owning several salons up north. Darrell asked about my life and children. I confided in him and confessed my fear of living illegally in the United States. At the time, he was the only person I felt I could trust, not to mention that I was attracted to him somewhat. Darrell was friendly and trusting in return. He shared about his ten-year-old son, David, whom he had custody of. Once again, I was crossing paths with a single parent.

My new friend invited me to meet his son. David was such an adorable young boy that he reminded me of my children whom I missed terribly. I was so worried about being deported that I told Darrell I was thinking of returning to Paris. That was when he offered to marry me.

The proposal came out of the blue. Although we weren't in love, we were adults and good friends. He knew he was doing me a favor. Before I could answer, he said, "You'd do the same for me, yes?" We were two lonely people who had a connection. I realized this would be a good way to avoid deportation.

Darrell and I moved into a bungalow on the canal, while Alain continued working with Ron in Key Largo and stayed on the rented houseboat. My new friend was a gentleman and a very attentive father. I found a job cooking in an Italian restaurant in the Little Italy section of Marathon, fifty-four miles southwest of Key Largo. By now I was pretty confident in my culinary skills.

Preparations were made for our marriage. My friend, Danielle, and her husband came down from Montreal to visit and assist with our wedding. Soon after, I received my Social Security number and a new last name. I was happy and feeling reassured.

We'd been married just a couple of months when Darrell told me David's mother was coming to the Keys on vacation. Her intent was to discuss financial matters. Darrell was in big trouble financially and was receiving letter after letter of notices, past-due bills, and the like.

His ex demanded we pay for vacations for both her and David whom Darrell had adopted when they'd married. I recognized she was putting the squeeze on him, so I helped Darrell with his finances and paid one of his debts, but I refused to fund vacations for his ex-wife and adopted son.

It was an uncomfortable situation. She wanted her husband back, and they had unfinished business to take care of. She was David's mother, and I felt bad being in the middle of their challenges.

Although we had only been married for three months, I believed it was important to get a separation and then a divorce. Darrell was miserable but agreed. He told me he'd apply for a divorce.

I was lost, very sad, and ashamed. So, I shared the news with my mom, talking to her on the phone and explaining US immigration rules.

Once again, I was on my own and had to decide what to do next. Marsha had moved into an apartment at the marina in Key Largo. She and Alain were preparing for their wedding. I told them my circumstances, that I was getting a divorce, and that I wished to move back to the houseboat. Instead,

Ron Wood offered me a room in his house along with a part-time job in his office. That was good, since I needed some ready cash so my children could visit me occasionally.

I also searched for another part-time job and heard about a famous restaurant in the Florida Keys. People referred to it as The Conch; it was considered the best eatery in the Keys and had a wildly colorful history.

Today, The Conch is called Ziggie & Mad Dog's. Over the years, many interesting personalities were involved with it, which wasn't surprising considering the numerous eccentrics who made the Florida Keys their home throughout the years.

The structure of The Conch was originally built as part of a pineapple plantation. Ziggie Stocki purchased the property in 1962 for a hundred grand, and the legendary Conch was born. The name was later changed when professional football player and Miami Dolphins great Jim "Mad Dog" Mandich got involved in 2005 and bought the place with his longtime business partner. They renovated it with great care and made it a celebration of great food, drink, and life in the Florida Keys.

Prior to Ziggie owning the restaurant, the property was infamous for tales of gamblers and shady characters. There were stories of Al Capone participating in high-stakes card games and other casino action in the back of the building. Ziggie was reportedly a notorious gambler himself. John Huston, the great film director, supposedly got the idea for his movie *Key Largo* while gambling at a casino Ziggie was known to frequent.

I was taking something of a gamble myself when I strode into the restaurant to see the manager. It was still called The Conch then and had a FINE FOOD neon sign along with the ZIGGIE YOUR HOST in bright electric script, as well as a non-working player piano built in the shape of a boat.

The staff was busy setting up lunch. "Where can I find the manager?" I inquired.

Someone gave me directions to an office behind the kitchen. Seated at a desk was an older lady, probably in her late sixties. She eyed me with slight interest.

"I'm looking for a waitress job," I told her.

"Our restaurant doesn't have openings," she briskly informed me. This was Virginia, widow of Ziggie Stocki. Her dog was asleep in his bed at her feet. Virginia looked like someone who managed herself and her restaurant well and didn't like to waste time.

But I wasn't someone to give up easily.

"Our employees have been working for us for years," she added.

"That's the reason I'm here. I want to work for the best!"

She smiled for the first time and handed me an application. Maybe I'd finally found a good job. Sure, I never did meet Ziggie, but I did encounter his widow—the right person to impress.

Virginia hired me and asked if I'd be interested in enrolling in medical insurance, one of the benefits the restaurant offered to employees. I gladly accepted, needing very much to see a doctor and follow the recommendation my Montreal physician had given me.

Soon, I was earning a very good income, mostly in tips. Anyone who's worked in the restaurant industry knows the weekly paycheck is the bare minimum. But at Ziggie's the tips were above average, thanks mainly to our clients, who were usually travelers and people on vacation.

39

Another Chance Encounter

When I look back on my life, I can't help but notice the many amazing twists my journey took. Some of the people I met seemed to come along at just the right time for me to go in a new direction. The next path occurred when I met Murray Sams, a powerful and prominent attorney.

It was early, before noon, and I was working at The Conch. A couple was seated at one of my tables. I approached and said, "Welcome to The Conch. Would you like anything to drink?"

After the man told me his order, the lady gave me hers, then asked, "Could you tell me where the restroom is?"

I gave directions, and she left. When I brought the drinks, I noticed she hadn't returned. I waited a few minutes to give her a chance to come back, but after a while, the man she'd come with was clearly becoming agitated. Approaching, I smiled and asked, "Do you want me to check on her?"

"Yes, please! That would be very good."

"Hopefully, she didn't fall in," I joked.

He laughed at that.

I found her in the restroom and casually asked, "Are you all right?"

She glanced at me, then said, "We drove all the way from Miami in a convertible."

No wonder she was taking so long in the restroom. She had to fix her hair and makeup!

The woman returned to her table, and I took their food orders. When I brought their meals, the man struck up a conversation with me. "You have an accent. Where are you from?"

"I was born in Morocco to French and Spanish parents."

"How interesting!" he remarked. "I just came back from France. I bought some Charolais cows. I wish I'd known you then. You could've helped me with my French." He smiled slyly.

I returned the smile while quietly and politely serving them both. But the man kept on asking me questions. "So where do you live? Did you have any children?"

I was getting nervous. For a moment, I feared he worked for the immigration authorities, but I kept my composure and diverted the subject away from me. "I've noticed horse and cow ranches around Ocala and wondered what it would be like to work on one." That elicited another smile from the man.

The couple had a fantastic lunch. They were happy and affectionate. On their way out, the man came up to me and put a big tip in my hand along with a business card. "My name's Murray Sams. My phone number's on my card. Call me if you want a job on the ranch."

As they strolled out, I was shaking. Was the universe once again trying to tell me something?

I kept my chance meeting with one of Florida's most important attorneys to myself for a couple of days but eventually told Ron, Alain, and Marsha, who agreed it wasn't safe for me to associate with Murray Sams. They warned me to be careful. However, I had good instincts, and my life experiences had taught me to be cautious. Nevertheless, though on guard, I was interested in Mr. Sams.

The address on the business card was for a corporate office building on Flagler Street in Miami. I drove there by myself merely to see it. It was a tall building, and Murray's office was on the top floor. I took the elevator all the way up. The doors opened, and I peered out at the offices of attorney Murray Sams, Jr., but didn't get out. Fear gripped me. *Not yet*, I thought.

I returned home and mustered up the courage to dial the attorney's office number. A receptionist answered and took a message. Murray soon returned my call and agreed to meet me at his office the following day.

Once again, I drove to Miami, but this time I met with the man. It was all very impressive. He introduced me to his personal secretary and a couple of his employees. Apparently, he had already mentioned me to them, and they encouraged me to take the job "the boss" was offering.

Murray told me about his ranch. "It's in Volusia County near the City of Deland. My son, Murray the Third, was the manager but felt called to something else. He lives in the Bahamas. Married a native. I confess he did a very poor job!"

I was already thinking to myself that this man, powerful and direct, might be a challenge. Still, people like him were often very successful in business.

He laid out the pitch. "I'd like you to live near the ranch and help me make some positive changes."

All right, okay! I found myself getting excited. *Is this really happening? Maybe I'm dreaming!*

"How much do you expect to be paid?" he asked. "I'll give you a truck, a house in Deland to live in, and all expenses paid."

I thought for a moment. "How about $500 per week net?"

"Okay! We've got a deal!"

And just like that I was hired.

"Meet me here tomorrow morning eight sharp," he said. "You and I will fly in my plane so you can see the ranch first from above."

This man wasn't messing around and wasn't about to waste any time.

"My daughter lives in Deland, and we'll meet her and her children. They'll pick us up at the Daytona airport and drive us to Swampwater Oak Ranch at Lake Ashby."

Events were happening fast, but so far I was comfortable with the deal. In the back of my mind, I kept the thought to keep my guard up. But this certainly was exciting!

Murray and I met the next day at the private executive airport in Miami. Standing next to his plane was his pilot, who welcomed us. It was a first for me. The freedom and flexibility of private jet travel was unparalleled. I was impressed.

We flew over Deland, allowing me to get an aerial tour of Murray's properties. As we jetted over Lake Ashby, I thought about snakes. There were a lot of them in Florida. I was an animal person, but snakes were certainly on my list of creatures I didn't like.

Landing at the Daytona Beach airport, we then drove to the ranch. There was a small cottage, but it hadn't been kept up. Murray hoped to renovate it in the near future. In the meantime, he'd bought an Airstream trailer to use as my office.

When I returned to Tavernier that same night, my friends were impatient to hear about my new job. "What's it really like?" they all wondered.

As I told them about my day, they thought I was joking. I guess it did sound too incredible. But it was real. However, I was worried about everything and tried to talk myself out of the job.

In my conversations with Murray, I'd expressed a strong desire to do something I really aspired to, something I loved. I felt I'd never had that kind of opportunity. He believed I could do the job, but I still had my doubts. I knew next to nothing about ranching, which was scary. I wanted to be successful and fretted about what would happen if I failed.

"You offered me this opportunity real quick," I said. "My friends question that. How could you decide so fast to give me such a good job with benefits?"

He flashed a confident smile, as good as a wink, then said, "I'm a criminal lawyer. When people are on the witness stand, I have to learn in a few minutes what they're like, whether or not they're telling the truth. That's my job! And I know you can do this. Your friends are idiots."

Of course, I knew my friends were just looking out for me. They were concerned. But Murray had boosted my confidence and helped calm me.

We met one more time in his residence. The dwelling looked more like a cathedral than a house. Big windows presented a splendid view of the water. It was a beautiful and very private place.

I was shown to the dining room. Murray was at the end of the table surrounded by several people. A delicious dinner had been prepared. He offered me a chair and introduced me to his guests. We ate and chatted, and I felt welcomed.

As I gazed out one of the large windows, I noticed a woman doing laps in the swimming pool. She was young, perhaps in her early thirties, but quite fit. She looked like a teenager. This was Mabel, Murray's second ex-wife. She had no interest in joining our lunch and ignored us.

There was one more thing I needed to take care of before I accepted the ranch job. It was a health concern. My doctor in Montreal had warned me about one of my ovaries. He'd told me an ovarian cyst was the cause of my pain and bloating. I was uncomfortable and had a fever and had to get it checked out!

When I spoke to Virginia at The Conch, she helped me with the health insurance, which I discovered would cover the surgery. I wanted to get it done immediately so I could start my new job in Deland.

Fortunately, Murray was understanding when I asked for a month before starting work. My new boss also knew I was an illegal alien, and I found comfort knowing he was a powerful attorney who could get me out of trouble with immigration if I got caught.

I also worried what I'd do if there was an accident or even a death in my family. Mom was living in Paris. My two children were in Montreal. What if I had to go to them for any reason? I could fly out but would be unable to re-enter the country. I'd already been in the United States more than six months, and my tourist visa had expired.

My heart wanted more than anything to live in the United States, and now I had what I believed would be a dream job. I knew what it was like elsewhere. After all, I had lived in four countries and dealt with dangerous situations and many challenges. Now I was finally in the United States but could be in trouble with the law.

I did feel a bit guilty about my situation, but my dream of becoming an American was getting closer. I'd do whatever it took to achieve that goal. Certainly, it was going to be difficult. I knew that. I wasn't born with a stamp that said AMERICAN CITIZEN, but I'd chosen to become one and was prepared to pay the price.

My surgery was done at a Miami hospital. It went well, and the recovery was short. Fortunately, the doctors didn't find cancer, but they did remove one ovary.

I spent a couple of weeks at Ron's place in Key Largo, resting and healing. Lying on a hammock or floating in the saltwater helped, and soon I got my strength back.

40

Ranching Florida-Style

Murray Sams gave me a truck to drive. It was 232 miles to Deland. I invited my friend, Mimi, to come along and keep me company. We'd met in the Keys and had become friends after spending time together snorkeling and diving for lobsters. I asked her to accompany me and be my driving partner. Mimi was interested in my new ventures but a little concerned, so I offered to pay for her return on a Greyhound bus. It was good to have her along.

We arrived in Deland, checked into a downtown hotel, and waited for Murray. He'd been born in this town and loved the ranching lifestyle. Sally, his first wife, still lived here, and she came to meet us at the hotel. She was a lovely person and gave us a warm welcome.

Murray had faith in me. But I was sure the rest of his family was concerned and wondered about the Frenchwoman. I was grateful to be given this big opportunity and recognized the responsibility. So I was determined to do my best and prove to his family that I was the right choice for the job.

I'd dropped Mimi off the day before at the bus terminal. Alone in the hotel room, I found myself full of anxious and excited thoughts about the next day.

Sunday morning came, and the phone rang at 6:00 a.m. I picked up the receiver and heard Murray's voice. "I'll be in Deland to pick you up at eight. Be ready!"

Yes, sir! I thought. I jumped into the shower and, as the water poured over me, excitedly realized this was really happening. My first day on this new job was about to commence.

On the drive to the ranch, Murray talked about what he expected me to do. The Airstream trailer had been set up close to the barn and would serve as my office.

"First thing you have to do," he instructed, "is contact the state's agricultural department and talk to an extension agent. They'll help you with the cows."

I was grateful for the advice. This was a new world for me, taking care of cattle and all. I knew I'd need help.

Murray continued. "You'll have to get a couple of local men to help get the work done. My daughter can give you suggestions. And she'll assist you with the payroll and weekly expenses."

We walked all morning, touring the ranch. When we got close to the herd of cows, he told me how his son had introduced a Brahman bull into it, which was a huge no-no. Murray had spent a fortune on his Charolais cows, up to $30,000 for some of them.

"Getting that bull out of there is a priority!" he said with emphasis. "It's not a good idea to mix breeds."

I discovered that Brahman bulls were mainly used for breeding and the meat industry. They originated in India and had a good tolerance for tropical conditions that fitted right in with Florida's climate. Maybe Murray the Third had meant well, thinking the bull would be good for growing a herd of beef. But clearly, his father thought differently.

I took notes for reminders; then we left the ranch and headed back to Deland. Murray had to return to work in Miami, so he flashed me a grin and wished me luck. "I'll be back next weekend!" he shouted as he got into his car.

Thus began my life as a rancher—me and my dog, Tina. We were the new management of Swampwater Oak Ranch.

Monday came, my first full day on the job, and Murray's son met me shortly after I arrived. He was a handsome young man and very friendly. The son had moved to the Bahamas because he wanted to live the Caribbean island life and only returned to help with the transition of a new manager. Nevertheless, I could sense he found it funny that his dad had given his job to a woman. It made me wonder what he was really thinking. But he was helpful and gave me a few tips, including where I could hire some ranch hands.

During my first week on the job, I contacted a Florida agriculture extension agent and told him I worked for Murray Sams. Saying his name was like pronouncing magic words. Right away, I got answers to my questions and support for what I needed. The agent showed up the very same day.

I kept notes on each animal in the herd, and pictures were taken to ID all of them. I was learning a lot. New words—*heifers*, *bulls*, and *steers*—became part of my vocabulary. My English was limited at times, but I always found it easy to learn new languages, another benefit of my past.

People unfamiliar with the cattle world might find it confusing. I'd always used *cow* as a blanket term. But now I became familiar with the difference between a cow and a heifer or a bull and a steer. Heifers were young female cows that had yet to give birth. Cows developed udders and became milk producers.

A steer was a male with its testes removed. Bulls, on the other hand, weren't neutered and could be tough or gentle. Each one was different, but all bulls were potentially dangerous. So it was wise to be wary and to respect all bulls, especially the ones that serviced dairy cows. They weren't to be trusted. Bulls were also strong. On any given day, they could turn and severely injure or even kill a person, young or old, inexperienced or experienced.

A couple of days passed, and I was given the keys to the house in Deland, which was owned by Murray. Here was where I'd make my home in the midst of an orange grove. I bought a bed and a couple of pillows for me and Tina.

That first week went by quickly. On Sunday morning, I got a call from Murray. He was coming to check on me. No problem.

A lot of work had been done, and I was proud of myself. Why not? This was a big challenge, and I believed I'd accomplished what I needed to do. I'd hired a couple of cowboys and been given recommendations for Murray's cows. A quick study, I learned what nutrients to give each animal and also how to be safe around them.

Murray arrived, and after telling him all I'd done, he appeared pleased. I breathed a sigh of relief. Then he asked, "Did you get that Brahman bull out of the ranch?"

"The bull's still with the cows and —"

He didn't let me finish. "I told you it was a priority. You should've gotten that son of a bitch out!"

I started shaking but didn't want to cry in front of him. This wasn't good. My first meeting with him so he could check my work and he was disappointed. Still, he calmed down really fast. On the other hand, I didn't.

That night I was in anguish. What to do? First of all, the bull was huge and mean. He wouldn't let anyone come into the pasture. His name was Rambo, which fitted him well.

Monday morning arrived, and I knew I had to find a way to get Rambo off Murray's place. I went to a neighbor's ranch, which belonged to a Mr. King. I knocked on his door, and when he answered, offered to give him the Brahman.

He laughed. "I got no safe place to keep him. Besides, I know that bull and want no part of him!"

"Please, you've got to help me," I begged.

"Why don't you kill him and grind up the meat?" he suggested. "Give it away as a donation."

Before he changed his mind, I agreed. "But just help me with it," I pleaded.

We drove to Murray's ranch, and there before my very eyes, I watched him shoot this big, beautiful animal. It hurt, but it had to be done. That was one of the hardest things I had to do as part of my job on the ranch.

It took me a whole week to calm down. But when the next Sunday arrived, Murray called to let me know he was on his way to visit.

I didn't tell him about the bull until he arrived at the ranch. He was in my office in the Airstream trailer when I let him know. "Your bull is no more."

He was clearly startled. "What do you mean the bull's no more?"

"I had Rambo killed and ground into hamburger."

"You did not!" he exclaimed.

"Yes, I did!" I could tell he was impressed. Being tough was part of the job, and from that day on, he realized I was on the same page as him.

I'd never met anyone quite like this man. Murray was an authoritarian leader with absolute control over his subordinates. He always maintained total decision-making power, and I worried how I'd survive with such a tough boss.

What I learned was to focus on my work, do my best, not let any of his feedback affect me, and not take whatever he said personally. He was paying me quite well. Besides, I actually liked his style—direct and no-nonsense.

The men I'd hired were in their twenties. They were family men, married and reliable, true cowboys. I enjoyed having them around but had to stay on guard against any stealing. Unfortunately, in the past there had been some abuses at the ranch. Past hands had stolen things such as feed and hay.

Part of the reason I was hired was to stop the abuses of the past and control the spending. Murray wasn't kidding around. It was a serious business for him in which he was investing a lot of money and time. In addition to the feed for the animals, I had to purchase gas, diesel fuel, and tools.

Also, there was a temptation for some of the cowboys to do things like grow marijuana, which at the time was quite illegal and could get the ranch into a lot of trouble if anyone was caught. It wasn't unusual for planes and helicopters to fly over the ranch searching for illegal pot fields.

I admired the cowboys. They liked to hunt. Every day at noon, they cooked up some kind of fresh meat on a grill—deer, squirrels, even snakes. They often shared it with me. I'd never been taught to eat snakes, but the cowboys showed me how to kill and consume them.

Of the various native species of snakes in the United States, thirty-five were in central Florida. I learned to be careful. Tina, my boxer, was my protector. She never left my side and warned me when she sniffed snakes.

After removing Rambo from the ranch, my next big job was to deal with the cows. Some of them had calves, and it was necessary to separate them and bring them to market. We had a number of offspring of mixed breed Charolais-Brahman, a no-no for Murray. I realized they had to go before he came back and threw another fit.

The two cowboys were able to get this job done while I kept notes and an inventory of the herd. They used a livestock head catch, the kind often found on a squeeze chute. That provided additional safety for those handling cattle and could be mounted on adjustable cattle alleys. The animals had to walk through the line into the chute where their necks got trapped. Then they could be inspected before we sent them to market.

Dr. Matson, the local veterinarian, was a lifesaver! He was a great country vet and a good Christian family man. I was grateful for his invaluable assistance.

Every month a technician paid a call to fill our tank of bull sperm with dry ice. We had some of the best bull semen and used it for artificial insemination of the cows, but it was also sold to those who wanted it. This was already part of the business before I was hired. However, Murray wanted a purebred Charolais bull for breeding his cows.

That was how Hannibal came to live on the ranch. He'd been brought over from France and kept quarantined for a year in Canada until he passed inspection, which was necessary to ensure he didn't have any diseases.

Hannibal was a big boy with a ring in his nose. He was well domesticated and had been hand-fed. Very docile and gentle, he was completely unlike Rambo. Still, he was a bull and couldn't be trusted. We had to be very careful around him.

Part of my job was to drive along the fence line of the ranch and keep an eye out for anything unusual. I kept a good pair of binoculars and a shotgun in my truck. And, of course, my trusted companion, Tina, was always with me.

When the occasional helicopter flew low over our ranch looking for marijuana patches, I warned the cowboys. "Mr. Sams is checking on us. Better go somewhere else to grow your weed!"

My cowboys were good teachers. I learned how to shoot my gun for hunting. Also how to clean and cut the kill to get the meat. Soon, I was enjoying eating outside around a wood fire. The food tasted so much better—simply divine. I guess I was turning into a real cowgirl!

Murray's visits became easier and more enjoyable. He was a busy man, so weeks could go by before he returned to the ranch. But I was in communication with the head office when I needed something. I also met with his daughter every Friday in Deland to get the payroll for the cowboys.

Each day was busy, but when the sun went down, I returned to Deland, just thirty minutes away. My little wooden house was located at the entrance to the town—the peaceful sanctuary of my dreams! Here I was living my American life, and it was great. I joined a gym, met several local folks, and settled into my new life, preparing my home to welcome a visit from Bruno Junior.

My son was now twenty years old and enjoyed his visit to the ranch. He loved Tina, my faithful boxer. Bruno Junior had a new girlfriend and was still living with his dad. I told him I didn't want to return to Montreal and would go back to Paris if I couldn't solve my immigration status. There was no way I could leave the United States until I had my green card. When my son returned to Montreal, I missed him terribly. However, unlike me, he totally loved his life in the cold weather of Canada.

41

A Jekyll and Hyde Affair

Post-traumatic stress disorder (PTSD) isn't just something military combat veterans suffer. Anyone who's lived through something horrible, often violent and terrifying, can find it difficult to recover from such an experience. I'd certainly dealt with some hard experiences, and writing about them sometimes stressed me out. However, I found it was important and necessary to tell my story and share my truth.

Early on, while working with cattle at the ranch, I discovered I needed a good scale. Everything was measured by weight, but where to find such a scale? This was before the internet, so naturally I consulted a phone book and located a neighboring town where I could acquire one. I called and made an appointment with the technician. When he arrived, I greeted him in the barn.

"Hello, nice to meet you," the technician said. "My name's Richard Franks, but please call me Dick."

He was polite, even a bit shy, but handsome with a gleam in his eye.

Richard wore work overalls with his name DICK FRANKS sewn on the front. He was in his late thirties, had big green eyes, a huge smile, and salt-and-pepper hair and beard. Richard looked a little like Kenny Rogers, the singer, and made an excellent first impression.

Very quickly, I could tell he knew the ranching business. We talked about the options for a scale and prices. Before he left, he gave me catalogs and more information.

The next day, Richard called and asked if I'd made a decision about the scale. I told him I'd found a used one at a better price, but that didn't deter him. He returned the next day to see me, and I was pleased! Richard admitted the used scale was a good deal, and I called the office in Miami and got the okay to make the purchase.

A Vietnam War veteran, Richard was very helpful to me during the time I worked at Murray's ranch. He loved to tell jokes and had a good sense of humor. We hit it off right away. I never called him Dick but always referred to him as Richard. Maybe he secretly liked that.

He stayed for a while that day, and we talked. Before he left, he asked, "How did a Frenchwoman like you find a job on a cattle ranch in the middle of Florida?"

I laughed. "I prayed to God for a good job!"

Up to that time, I'd never been close to religion, so mentioning God was merely a habit. I believed in myself. I was strong and smart. But in my life I couldn't deny the spiritual things that happened to me. I recalled the miracle of a New Year's Eve on a desolate road in Manitoba when we ran out of gas. A trucker arrived out of seemingly nowhere, stopped, filled our tank, and then drove off without a word. Angels were truly among us!

It seems I was attracted to spirits, both good and bad. In fact, I was a spirit. Ultimately, all of us were. In the end, with proper belief, nothing was impossible. I even told Murray one day that I was afraid of nothing. Fear didn't live inside me. That attitude impressed him.

This strong belief in myself was necessary as I learned how to do the hard work the ranch required. Yes, I had cowboys to help me, but I was the boss. During this time, I also longed for something more—a friend or even a relationship.

Richard called me after several days and asked if he could take me to dinner. I agreed, and we met. I noticed he wasn't wearing a wedding ring, but he had the telltale sign on his finger—tan lines that revealed he must have worn one.

He vaguely mentioned that he was a single man again. I was also single. I shared with him about the short marriage to Darrell. He opened up and told me about his marriage and how he was getting divorced. She was his second wife, and he'd adopted her son. Richard never had children of his own but was paying child support for his ex-wife's boy. We ended up talking for hours about everything. I told him about my long life journey that had finally brought me to America to live my longtime dream.

Richard was proud to have served his country fighting in the Vietnam War. But like most people who experienced combat, he had troubling memories. Listening to the good music that had been current during that time helped. Music had played an important role for the men at war in the jungle.

Sometimes, however, when he told me about his war experiences, he got a very sad look on his face. I let him tell me about the hell the young men had gone through. It was horrible. During the Vietnam War, I was living in Canada and followed daily details in the news. It was apparent that America was suffering, with so many young men dying or coming back injured and broken. Because the war had become so unpopular, there was much protesting in the United States, making it even harder on those who returned home. In many cases, there were no hero welcomes. Often just the opposite. Such an unkind cut.

On Murray's next visit to the ranch, I told him about Richard Franks. I was excited to share with him about this man who was about my same age, handsome, good around animals, and hands-on every time I needed help. Not only was he experienced with cow birthing, but he was a knowledgeable and fun outdoorsman. He was a bass fisherman, deer hunter, dog lover, and more!

My boss wanted to meet him. At the ranch, I introduced them to each other. The meeting was positive.

Murray remarked, "I'm getting two managers for the price of one!"

Soon, Richard frequently stayed with me. He also introduced me to his family, who were good Christians and prayed often. His parents adored their son and gave him great support.

I hadn't been in a church since my primary school years. I didn't even know my prayers in English. But Richard's parents were so kind. They were truly wonderful people and very accepting when they learned that Richard and I planned to get married.

I fell in love for the second time in my life. The first was Bruno, the father of my children. I was so young then, just seventeen years old. This time I was older and with a handsome man in his late thirties. It was fantastic to love and be loved. I didn't think I'd ever really have such a feeling again.

I needed a green card and hired the best immigration attorney in Daytona Beach. First, Richard and I had to get married. For some reason

I don't recall, we were wedded in Georgia in front of a judge. There was something about the rules in Florida.

Murray seemed genuinely happy for me and respected the job I was doing. We became good friends. He even trusted me to discuss his romantic life. Murray had met a young lady and was planning to start a family with her. She had never been married and wanted to have children. By then, Murray was in his sixties but refused to be an old man. It gave him great joy when he became the father to a precious little girl. Later, he had another girl and a boy.

Eventually, the whole family visited the ranch, but they didn't like life on it. Murray, though, enjoyed his new life very much. Wanting to impress his family, he purchased two quarter horses. Both were pregnant, which led to more horses!

I'd never ridden a horse but soon learned. Fortunately, the two mares were very patient with me and even let me ride them bareback. It was a real thrill, and before long, I was an enthusiastic rider. I loved them so much that my affection for them soon surpassed my love for the cows.

Since Murray's new family wasn't keen about ranch life, he often came alone, brought female friends with him, and spent a relaxing time in the country. He loved the forest of tall trees on Lake Ashby. There were also numerous Indigenous burial mounds. And, of course, snakes!

The lady visitors were terrified of serpents and asked me to come along to reassure them. Every time they hid behind me. The sight of a snake was obviously the stuff of their nightmares—for me, too, until I learned how to watch for them carefully and where to place my feet when sitting down. Snakes could be under rocks or logs. If a rattle was heard, it was important not to jump or panic. I learned to locate where the sound was coming from before attempting to move.

A good pair of boots was a must. Murray's ladies weren't prepared—they were city folks. I had to laugh to myself. It hadn't been that long ago that I was inexperienced and a bit naive about country life, too.

Richard and I grew closer and worked together on the ranch, but we also desired a place of our own. We found a fifteen-acre property for sale in Lake Ashby. It was close by, just a few minutes from the ranch.

It belonged to an older couple who agreed to hold the mortgage while we made payments. Richard's parents lent us the down payment. This was a good arrangement that worked well for our situation.

We moved out of the wooden house in Deland. Living at our own little ranch by Lake Ashby gave us great enjoyment. Richard seemed to be the husband I'd always dreamed of, the perfect mate, and our first four years together were blissful and happy.

Richard and I made a few trips together to Montreal to visit my children. What a blessing to see Murielle and Bruno Junior. They were becoming young adults. Before long, in 1984, Murielle's daughter, Melanie, was born. She was my first grandchild! Of course, I flew back to Montreal to welcome her into my life.

Visiting my children and my new granddaughter in Montreal was wonderful, but Canada was still no place for me. I truly enjoyed my life in Florida. An avid fisherman and hunter, Richard taught me a lot about the outdoors. We caught bass and hunted deer, prestigious catches for those who appreciated wildlife.

I was surprised at another talent Richard possessed. He loved art and oil painting and was quite good at it, so much so, in fact, that I asked him to teach me. It was something I wanted to learn and was also a way I could show him appreciation.

Richard agreed to help me and even decided to find a teacher for us. Mr. E.B. Stowe turned out to be a great discovery. He was a wonderful artist and a wise old man. His studio was on the shore of the Saint John River. We met him there every Saturday morning at nine for lessons from him.

Soon, our art teacher was visiting me at the ranch. I drove him around for hours, which he loved, especially the horses. He also wanted to visit the palm forest where there were many ancient Indigenous mounds. His way of thanking me for these tours was to paint me a beautiful picture of huge palms. Such a treasure!

In addition to our shared love of painting and art, Richard wanted to teach me to shoot. First, it was with a shotgun. Later, he bought me a rifle cut to my arm length. Thanks to these lessons, I learned to handle guns, even became something of a huntress, which gave me self-confidence and pride at learning this skill.

In our early years together, Richard and I lived a great life, one I'd dreamed of. But it didn't last. Before long, dark clouds gathered on the horizon. Storm clouds approached that soon altered our relationship.

Richard told me he didn't drink, that alcohol was poison to him, that it had destroyed his marriage. It also brought back bad memories of the Vietnam War. So it was an unpleasant surprise the day he came home smelling like beer.

There was little indication he'd begun drinking again except that I noticed he'd become belligerent and impatient. I was worried and started calling my mom frequently, sometimes several times per day. She didn't believe someone could get drunk on beer alone, but I wasn't so sure.

"He's on something," I told my mother. "Maybe it's drugs."

Richard became a different person from night to morning. After snapping at me the evening before, he apologized and begged for forgiveness in the morning. Something was up! I became suspicious that he was drinking behind my back. It bothered me that he was hiding it, so I had to ask. After our first years of happiness, something had changed and I wanted to know what it was, what was upsetting him.

Eventually, I confronted him. "What's going on with you? Something's not right. What's happening with you?"

He confessed to drinking beer. "It relaxes me in the evenings."

"You promised me you'd never drink again."

That was how it went with someone with a drinking problem. Denial to others and to themselves, and an obsession and craving that couldn't be conquered without help.

Fortunately, his parents were supportive. I reached out to them and they responded with helpful support. They were always so sweet to me and accepted me with love and kindness. They, too, were concerned for their son. My mother-in-law told me how her father had been an alcoholic and had made his family very unhappy. She was also a nurse and was against excessive drinking because she understood its negative effects.

Richard could be very loving and kind when he was sober. But eventually the drinking came to a head; recalling what happened still breaks my heart.

One day, I came home for lunch. The phone rang, and I answered it. The lady on the other end identified herself, and I recognized her as the manager of the store where we rented movies.

"You need to return some overdue movies Mr. Franks rented," she demanded.

I immediately apologized. "So sorry. Can you tell me the titles?" Her response surprised me. They sounded like X-rated movies. "Are you certain?

It must be a mistake. We've returned all our rentals." I didn't understand. When we bought our first VCR player, we often rented movies from that store. We were good customers, and I wasn't aware of any past-due rentals.

After I hung up the phone, I started thinking about it. We watched movies together. But I knew that Richard often continued after I went to bed.

I ate my lunch and kept thinking about it, getting more and more upset. Evening came, and Richard arrived home. I came out to greet him but paused as he locked his truck. I decided to wait to say anything until we were in the kitchen. Taking a big breath, I asked, "I got a call today from the video store. The woman said you haven't returned three movies. Three X-rated ones."

Richard turned crimson. "You told me you didn't want to watch porn, but I do!"

I walked away. All these nights he was staying up and watching those films. He was very upset that I'd found out about them. Well, I was upset, too. In fact, I was hurt and so angry I didn't talk to him anymore that night and just went to bed.

After that, things were much tenser between us. I was always the first to arrive home to our Lake Ashby ranch. My days were full of hard work. One day, I was particularly tired and went to bed. Suddenly, I was awakened by screaming. It was late, around midnight.

Richard stormed into the bedroom, turned on the light, and came to my side of the bed. I'd been asleep for hours and was groggy. He grabbed my throat and squeezed hard. I was choking and fought back, begging him to let me go. Finally, he released his grip and left the room, all the while yelling and cussing!

He'd left the light on, so I got up, opened the closet door, grabbed my shotgun, turned off the light, and went back to bed. I was ready to protect myself if necessary.

A few minutes later, he returned, screaming nasty swear words. He switched on the light and saw me facing him with the gun pointed right at him. He backed up and put both hands in the air. "Don't shoot! Oh, God, I'm begging you, please don't kill me."

It was a pitiful sight, but I could no longer trust him. I knew the feeling of being a victim. "How does it feel, huh? You assaulted me!"

"I'm sorry!" he said, walking slowly backward into the hallway. It all happened in a few seconds but felt as if it was in slow motion. He backed his way into another bedroom, closed the door, and locked it.

"Don't you ever put your hands on me again!" I shouted through the door, kicking it with my foot for good measure. He was drunk but knew I was serious, since he locked himself in another room.

At daybreak, I left the ranch. I needed to talk to someone, so I called Mom. All of the anguish and heartbreak spilled out.

"What do you have to lose?" she told me. "It's best to keep your dignity and self-respect. Please let him go! You owe it to yourself for your health and peace of mind."

As usual, she was right. I was so grateful for a mother who stood by my side, even when we were separated by thousands of miles. All the way across the ocean from Paris, her motherly love and concern were expressed to me.

The fight with Richard was a serious matter, so I stayed in my office at the ranch. I might have been fearless, but I wasn't foolish. It was important to have some space and to stay away from him until things cooled down.

After a couple of days, Richard contacted me and told me I should stay in our home. He wasn't there and was staying with Mr. Stowe, our art teacher and good friend. That reassured me. We'd known Mr. Stowe for some time and loved to be around him. Both of us had painted with him for a couple of years, usually on Saturdays, always learning from him and developing our techniques.

It had been good to talk to Mom, but I knew I needed more than long-distance care, so I called a therapist friend of mine. My heart broken, I was crying out for help. I'd spent four of the best years of my life with Richard, and now it was over.

My therapist told me that many war veterans were damaged, which was especially true for Vietnam ones who had suffered so much from recurring memories of the atrocities they'd experienced. A lot of them had turned to drugs and alcohol to tame their minds and seek relief. I didn't know what medications Richard might have been on, but I certainly knew he'd changed.

He'd shown me that he was a man of many talents. We'd had a good time together. But after what had happened that night, there was no way I could trust him again. When I closed my eyes, I felt his hands around my neck. Such memories terrified me.

Once again, it was time for a change.

42

Café de France

My good fortune over the years in working in restaurants turned out once again to be beneficial. I'd made a few friends in Florida, one of whom lived in Orlando, where she worked in real estate. She called one day to tell me about a little French restaurant in Winter Park that was for sale. She knew I'd owned La Marguerite in Montreal. As it turned out, this was good timing, and I was very interested.

I'd always hoped my children might come to live in America. Bruno Junior had graduated from a pastry class in Montreal and was searching for work. I was able to get him a green card and also procured one for both Murielle and my granddaughter, Melanie. I discussed the plan with Bruno Junior and Murielle, and they seemed keen to move to Winter Park and work at my new restaurant. Their father, Bruno Senior, even agreed to lend them half the down payment to close the deal for the café, making them part owners, since I'd control the other half.

It took several weeks to negotiate the purchase of Café de France. The lady selling the business was from France and had to return there after a relationship breakup. This seemed like a wonderful opportunity, especially getting my children to be part of it. But my kids still needed encouragement, and fortunately, my brother Alain was able to join us for a couple of months as we got started.

Running a restaurant was hard work and took time to build into profitability. So Bruno Junior and Murielle had to live on a shoestring budget, while Alain couldn't stay in the United States and eventually returned to Paris.

Working for Murray Sams had been rewarding. It was a good job, but after seven years and all that had happened, it was time for a change. I needed that income, but this was a chance to reunite with my children. Plus, I thought it would be good to have a family business.

I guess I was dreaming!

Luckily, the restaurant had employees from the previous owner who decided to stay with us. I wanted this to be something my children could share with me, so from the very first day, they were my equal partners. They worked the day shift, while I did 5:00 to 10:00 p.m. I picked up Melanie from the babysitter and took her to her mom's. Then I worked hard through the evening and closed up the operation at night, allowing my children to have evenings off.

Despite my best efforts at encouraging them, I soon realized my kids didn't really like the restaurant business. Their responsibilities were more than they were ready or willing to do. On top of that, their father made frequent visits, which was no help at all! Bruno Senior preferred life in Canada and always criticized the American way of life. So our children got conflicting views. I had to accept the reality that my children and I were disconnected.

Bruno Junior was dating a Canadian girl in Montreal who came for a visit and stayed with us for a couple of weeks. After her visit, Bruno told me he was going back to Montreal to be with her. Well, so long, my son! My children were now old enough to make their own decisions; both refused to continue working at the restaurant. They just weren't committed to it.

I'd spent seven years working for Murray Sams, an experience that had taught me a lot of things. I was proud of myself for all the work I'd accomplished. It had been more than just managing the ranch. Richard and I had bought and raised horses, and I assisted Murray with some of his own horses, which he'd purchased for his children to enjoy.

Over time, he'd added more responsibilities for me. I became the manager of his duplex rentals and also handled the harvest of his orange groves. Believe me, it was worth it; all those experiences taught me much more about running a business. I was able to apply those lessons and skills later in life. For now, it was time to tell Murray what I was doing.

"I've bought a restaurant in Winter Park called Café de France," I told him.

"What?" he said, clearly shocked. "But you work for me."

I tried to explain the situation to him. "When I left Montreal seven years ago, I was pursuing my dream of living and working in America. But I knew I'd let my children down. So, buying this restaurant is really for them, not me."

Judging by the disappointed expression on his face, Murray wasn't satisfied with my reason for purchasing the restaurant.

I kept working at the ranch for a time, doing my work, but I'd lost the will to remain. Part of this was the result of what had happened with Richard. I needed to get away and do something different. The restaurant prospect had come at the perfect time. It was just sad that I had a restaurant now in my name and my children didn't want any part of it, even though I'd told Murray I was doing this venture for them.

Obviously, I couldn't continue working both jobs. I had to make a decision. My heart told me what to do. It was always important to listen to one's heart and follow it as well as possible.

Murray came to say goodbye. "I want you to know, Janine, that if you change your mind about this restaurant business, call me."

I nodded. "Thank you for all you've done for me. Working for you was the best!"

After that, I gave the truck keys to Joe, the new manager, and walked away for good.

Murray had taught me so much. There was no doubt about that. He was a fantastic soul and a great teacher. I knew I'd miss talking to him. He was never boring!

Five years later, Murray met me one last time. "I made the worst mistake when I let you go." I'd earned his respect and was glad to close our friendly relationship without resentment. There was much to be thankful for in our time together, and I also really appreciated his family. They'd saved my heart when I needed it.

By then, I was living in Lake Ashby by myself and driving daily to Winter Park in a small Mercedes I'd bought for the commute. Richard and I weren't divorced yet, but when I talked to him about getting the divorce, he understood and agreed.

Before I left the house for the last time, I wrote on the blackboard next to the entrance to the kitchen: WELCOME TO THE HOUSE CALLED HELL. It was an impulsive thing to do and something I eventually regretted.

I was on my own again. Richard had crossed the line, so we stayed away from each other. He was the one who had taught me about guns, and then I had to use one to protect myself. The last time I saw him was in the courthouse when our divorce was finalized.

I'd lived like a bush woman and a cowgirl for seven years. Now here I was painting my nails, wearing high-heeled shoes, and becoming a city girl.

It was hard to accept that my dream of a family restaurant business wasn't going to happen. One morning, before driving to work, I cried out to God. I was down on the rug on my knees, me who had never addressed God for anything! I found myself praying as I'd never done before. "Why, God? Why? Am I being punished?" I let it all pour out of me. All I'd ever wanted was to reunite my family, but instead buying Café de France had divided us.

But I pulled myself together and did what I had to do. It helped that I was familiar with the restaurant's employees, having done the payroll myself and working evenings. I got to know Dominique, one of the waitresses and a friend of Murielle's. She couldn't understand why my daughter had left the restaurant. Dominique was an excellent employee whom I got along well with. She was young, in her early twenties, and went to school while she waitressed at night. And she was madly in love with a handsome Colombian man named German. He was also a student and delivered pizzas at night. Eventually, they became a team and got married.

From day one, I'd rolled up my sleeves and worked hard. Soon, I was enjoying the work. We had good customers and a relaxing ambience. I'd missed the restaurant life and was back at it. Everything was great: the cooking, the food, and providing good service to the customers.

One of my goals was to have an outside terrace in the space under the awning, something common with restaurants in France. I thought it would be wonderful for us. But when I applied for a permit, the City of Winter Park turned me down. It didn't allow service on the sidewalk, but I didn't let that stop me. I could be persistent and stubborn when necessary. After a lot of pushing, I got the first permit for a terrace in the city!

Soon things improved. The restaurant did better day after day. The people of Winter Park cherished an eatery that served delicious French food. Along with wine and beer, we also had a large selection of French pastries. It was all coming together and paying off as we developed an excellent clientele.

43

A Visit from Immigration

One day, immigration people came to our restaurant. They wanted to check for work visas. Thanks to Richard, I had a green card in good order, but it was a different story for some of my employees.

I had to close the restaurant for the night while the immigration officers talked to my workers and discussed next steps. Unfortunately, my chef and his wife were told they had thirty days to leave the country and return to France.

Dominique, my good waitress and friend, was able to get her papers in order. She returned a few weeks later. But I had to find another chef who, of course, had to be a French one. It wasn't easy dealing with the changes, but I managed.

I discovered someone had called US Immigration Services, tipping it off that illegals were working at Café de France. It could have been anyone, but I suspected it was Bruno, my ex-husband.

Murielle had moved to Fort Myers with Melanie, her daughter, and a friend. They'd been living with me for a year. and overnight, they were gone, leaving no forwarding address. It turned out that Bruno was spending time with them; sometime later he brought Melanie to Winter Park for a visit.

I was happy to see my granddaughter. I wondered, though, what Bruno was up to. He claimed he only wanted me to see Melanie, but in truth he was eager to see how I was managing the restaurant. Bruno couldn't stand not knowing what I was doing. This fed my suspicion that he was the one who had called Immigration Services. It might have been a vicious thought on my part, but I knew he hated seeing me successful.

Before too long, our clientele increased. Things had been running in the red, but we were able to turn it around and get our revenue in the black. I was proud of that, and my life got easier.

We had plenty of appeal for the people in the area. Our dining room featured traditional French bistro food served in a relaxed atmosphere.

Patrons could choose from an extensive wine list and dine either indoors or outdoors on the terrace, both providing great views of citizens passing by. White tablecloths, chic decor, immaculate service, fine dining music, and culinary muscle—a quality recipe for success.

44

Soulmates

The universe was strange and mysterious. I discovered that in my own life experiences. Some things couldn't be explained—miracles, angels, the "right thing in the right place at just the right time." However it was described, when these things beyond explanation happened, one could only accept them for what they were—gifts!

I'd had a few different relationships over the years, even married three times, though I could only say one was for true love. It seemed I was attracted to people in different ways. It wasn't always because my heart was drawn to them. Sometimes it was the naïveté of youth, a desire to connect, a longing for friendship, or simply the strong pull of lust.

If someone desired to help me, genuinely and honestly, that would open me up. Yes, I guarded my heart. Who wouldn't after my childhood and first marriage? Even a marriage I thought was for love turned sour. Richard had had too many demons to fight.

Could anything prepare me for what came next? I think my heart was always searching for that true love who would take me as I was, the good and the bad. It had to be a man who could see beyond my tough exterior and into the tenderness of my heart. I was fierce when I had to be. I'd learned that from my mother, but I also hoped someday to find a soulmate who would be kind, true, strong, and independent. That was the gift that came to me after several years of living and working in Florida.

Saturday nights were always busy at the restaurant. I worked behind the service bar, preparing beverages and taking care of credit-card payments. I was in charge and knew it, but it was good to have a dependable staff I could trust.

Thank goodness for Dominique. One Saturday evening, she approached me. "Could you meet me at Bob and Beverly's table?"

We all knew Beverly and Bob Borngesser, a very friendly couple and two of our best customers. They loved Dominique and wanted to introduce her to one of their single friends from Milwaukee, a Dr. John Winters. I guess Dominique was nervous and hoped I could assist in the situation.

He sat at the end of the table and got up when he saw me coming over. Standing, he smiled and introduced himself. "Hello, I'm John Winters from Milwaukee, Wisconsin."

I returned the smile. "Nice meeting you. Welcome to Café de France. I'm Janine."

He shook my hand. "Are you the chef tonight?"

"No, I'm not, but I prepare the wine, drinks, and desserts."

He smiled again. "Where are you from? I like your accent."

"It's French." Then I excused myself and returned to work behind the bar. The restaurant was full, and I didn't have time to chat.

At the end of their dinner, I joined their table and had more time to talk. They had enjoyed their leg of lamb with baby vegetables. Of course, I was pleased.

The next day, John paid me a visit, and every day after that. He came in for lunch, sitting at the service bar where he could talk to me while he ate. Soon, I knew a lot about this man. He was a radiologist in Milwaukee and had traveled there to spend time with his friends.

One day, when he came for lunch, I told him about the trouble we were having with the dishwasher. He asked for some tools and went to work. After a little while, he'd fixed the big stainless-steel machine.

I discovered he'd learned skills like that from his dad. His father was an electrical engineer and had often taken his son with him, teaching him the trade. A fascinating note was how John had helped his dad with the Empire State Building's lights when he was only fourteen years old!

After his two-week vacation was up, he returned to Wisconsin, but he called me daily. We talked about everything. I enjoyed getting his phone call each morning. It was a wonderful way to wake up. Soon, he was calling me at night when I got home from a long day at work.

John told me about his divorce two years earlier. I shared with him about my life, including my mistakes and also my hopes and dreams. He was so easy to talk to. Most of all, he was gentle and kind. We gave each other great comfort.

I started thinking about him all the time. I was aware of myself and my emotions, but I stayed grounded. Good energy was direct and positive, and I believed when one meditated on love, one's energy attracted it.

We became fast friends. There was no competition. Both of us were a bit uncertain where the relationship was going. What to do next? I didn't want to lose this newfound friendship! He gave me such reassuring comments, and I enjoyed his company, whether he was near or far away in Milwaukee.

I think he felt the same, and I could tell he was lonely. He didn't like the single life.

We'd been talking on the phone for weeks when John asked me to join him on Sanibel Island for a long weekend. Sanibel was a beautiful place just off the southwest coast of Florida in the Gulf of Mexico.

At first I told him no, but I hung up the phone and began thinking about his proposal. A few minutes later, I called him back. "Sorry! I changed my mind."

"No worries. I'll take you sailing."

I'd never sailed before but had always enjoyed watching sailboats—the way they utilized the wind to power them and change directions. I closed my eyes and felt comfort. I recalled the times on the beach in Morocco, gazing at the sea and watching the various boats serenely sailing. I realized something then. My life was shifting yet again.

At our age, we both knew our relationship had to be solid. No more nonsense. I'd had enough of that, and probably him, too!

His vacation was two weeks in the future. I didn't tell anyone I was taking a long weekend off. But every time I thought about it, my heart raced; I was anxious and happy at the same time. The closest we'd been physically was when we'd hugged before his return home. With this invitation, it was as if we were moving to a new phase in our relationship.

Café de France was my future. I badly wanted to be successful on my own and prove to my family that I could do it. Investing in the restaurant was a way to build something for me and my children, but they'd walked away. They couldn't see its potential, but I knew it was a good thing.

John was encouraging and supportive. It was a gradual process that began with his appreciation and grew into a great support of all my goals.

45

Our Sanibel Island Vacation

John flew to Orlando from Milwaukee. I arrived on time at the airport and nervously waited for him at the luggage pickup, hoping I'd recognize him among all the passengers. When I saw him, he came up to me, opened his arms, and gave me a big hug. It was such a warm welcome!

We walked to my car, and I unlocked the doors. Gently, he took the keys from my hand and said softly, "I'll be the driver."

I never let anyone drive me in my car, but I didn't say anything. He was such a gentleman.

On the way from the airport to Sanibel, I kept stealing glances to my left. John was just as happy as me, making jokes and smiling. We had many conversations, talking in detail about our hopes for the future. Being next to him was exciting!

John was a handsome man. His attractiveness went beyond his good looks. Kindness, dependability, and faithfulness—these were the things most women found turn-ons. He had all of those qualities along with moral integrity. I realized my first weekend in Sanibel would be spent with an angel.

We arrived at the island. It was beautiful, and my heart swelled at the sight. Our condo was located right on the beach. It was incredibly comfortable and even had a big swimming pool.

John had already made preparations for our next day. He'd rented a sailboat and was excited to take me out on the sea. Our plan was to spend the day sailing and have a picnic.

"I'll prepare the food," I told him. "You buy the wine."

We went shopping, and when we returned from the store, we had dinner at a local gourmet restaurant. The anticipation of being together grew with each moment. We were both excited and relished each other's company.

After dinner, I began preparing our picnic meal, using all my culinary skills. Jumbo steamed shrimp, chicken salad, a strawberry mango mesclun salad, hot pink lemonade, and chocolate truffles were on the menu.

John had bought two bottles of champagne that we kept nice and cold. Then we cleaned up the kitchen. By that time, we'd consumed several glasses of wine and were tired but happy.

The next day was the best of my life! My eyes were on John the whole time, watching him work the sails. He was clearly the master of the boat. It was adorable. The more I gazed admiringly at him, the more he smiled.

John was a tall man, over six feet, handsome and strong. He was in control, and I felt calm and confident in his presence. We sailed for a while, then found the island for our picnic. He lowered the sails and threw out the anchor. Stepping onto land, I was in total bliss. Such a beautiful day!

Another boat had also anchored, and four people were swimming. We also got in the water and enjoyed the warmth of the gulf, soaking in it up to our chins. Next was our picnic. The food was a hit, and the champagne was divine. Recalling it all was one of my treasured memories.

46

Meeting John's Family

I'd met hundreds of customers at Café de France, but not one had interested me. I wasn't looking just for a man in my life. What I wanted was a companion and a true bond. I needed someone I could share the rest of my life with. It was my hope and belief that there was a very special man who loved me the way I wanted to be loved.

It was a gradual process that began with appreciation and respect. Yes, I was attracted to John early on. But it was over time that our relationship grew into that special one I'd been seeking. We connected in many ways, perhaps because we'd both lived long enough to undergo the ups and downs that came with various relationships. Experience was a great teacher.

After our wonderful Sanibel weekend, it was back to Café de France. John continued to come daily for lunch. The two of us also went shopping or swimming at Bob and Beverly's place. But after a few days, it was time for John to return to his hospital in Milwaukee. He was one of seven radiologists at West Allis Hospital and very much appreciated.

John and I stayed in touch, phoning each other morning and night. After a few months, it was clear things were getting more serious. John offered to fly me to visit him in Milwaukee and meet his adolescent children.

Mike was twenty and recovering from a bad accident that had happened when he was in college in Louisiana. One night, he was drinking and ended up in a drunken altercation with another young man outside a pub. That man dragged him five blocks under his car! There were charges filed, and in the eventual settlement, Mike received a large financial settlement.

His younger sister, Beth, was still a teenager, about seventeen, and seemed to me to be spoiled and disrespectful. I understood. She was protective of her dad after his divorce and didn't want any woman around him. Beth was a loving daughter and didn't want to share her father with me.

The visit was fun with a lot going on. It was the Fourth of July holiday, and there was a big parade with lots of horses and other animals. Sure, it was summer then, but Milwaukee wasn't a pleasant town for me. It just didn't feel welcoming. I found the place too old and knew in the winter it would be too cold. We talked about that and my fear of the cold. John understood and was willing to do whatever it took to keep us together.

We'd known each other for six months when John asked me to marry him.

I called Mom to tell her about our engagement. "Why would you want to get married?"

She seemed genuinely surprised. I think after all I'd been through, she was just being a concerned parent.

"I want more than a lover," I told her. "I want a husband, a faithful one who loves me for who I am. I believe John's the one."

We all carried the energy of trauma along with the negative and positive experiences in our lives. John and I both had had previous marriages that didn't go well. But we were two good people and needed each other to continue our lives.

Men in love tended to see the best in their partners, maybe even viewing the other person more positively than themselves. Sometimes those deep romantic feelings found them holding idealized images of their partners. I trusted John, however, and felt safe in his company. He didn't judge me for my past and had suffered enough in his first marriage.

Mary was John's first wife, and they had adopted their children, Mike and Beth, from an orphanage in Chicago. John was a well-paid radiologist, and the kids were treated well. They had a good home with a private school education and material gratifications.

Over time, Mary had developed a drinking problem and become abusive, which led to the crumbling of their seemingly perfect life and eventually to divorce. Fortunately, Mary later found sobriety. They had been divorced for two years before I met John.

According to John, money wasn't a problem. He gave his ex-wife 50 percent in the divorce settlement, and she had remarried. The children were busy living their lives around friends and family in Wisconsin.

Children were an important part of our lives and were impacted by what we did as well as what happened from their own actions. All I could say was that I'd always felt it was right to be good to John's children and to help them when I could and truly required it. This was true of my own children, as well.

47

The Wedding at Café de France

John and I had a beautiful wedding in a church, followed by a celebration at Café de France. It made total sense to hold the reception there. The food was delicious, plus great drinks and friends in a family atmosphere. I was pleased that Murielle and Melanie could attend. Also present were Beth and Mike Winters. Mike brought along a friend, a lovely girl he was seeing at the time. Dominique and German were in charge of the party and did a great job.

We spent the night at the Hyatt in Orlando. The next week, we flew to Maui for a dream honeymoon in Hawaii. We stayed at the Sandals Hotel in Maui and enjoyed all kinds of activities. This was a trip fit for a queen! It was so fun to explore the beautiful Hawaiian Islands, do some snorkeling, and see impressive waterfalls, volcanoes, and unique wildlife. It was quite something to see humpback whales or sea turtles. We also marveled at the rare Hawaiian monk seal.

Especially impressive were the birds. The Hawaiian goose, the nēnē, is the rarest goose in the world. And I truly loved the ʻiʻiwi and ʻapapane, two birds that belong to the scarlet honeycreeper species.

I'd never been on a real vacation. Yes, I'd traveled to many continents, but it was the first time I could really enjoy myself and be so happy. I believed John was very pleased, too, and appreciated treating me so well. In addition to sightseeing, we played lots of backgammon, including some tournaments with the hotel's employees. John wasn't familiar with the game and tried hard to win, but I had the upper hand with my experience. It took him many attempts to finally beat me.

One of the highlights was a trip to Hana. This idyllic village on the eastern tip of Maui was at the end of the Road to Hana, also known as the Hana Highway. What a wonder it was with its lush greenery, botanical gardens, and historical sights. In the 1800s, Hana had boasted several sugar plantations. A sea captain named George Wilfong had established the first one in 1849 and had to hire Chinese laborers to work the fields when he was unable to get native workers. *Hana* means "labor" in the Hawaiian language.

Maui was a lovely tropical paradise. There were quiet beaches to visit away from the crowds and tourists. The fifty-two-mile drive with John at the wheel was a memory to treasure. The highway skirted the northern shore, and while on it, we saw amazing sights such as carpets of wildflowers and spectacular glimpses of the ocean. It was the ride of my life!

When we finally reached Hana, we spent time meditating on the beach. John turned to me. "Someday I'd like to sail here on our own boat. I'll call it *Queen Janine*."

"Oh, please don't call it that. I'm not a queen."

"You *are* my queen!"

John made it clear he didn't want me to work outside the home. We had enough money to live comfortably. Although I'd worked all my life, I loved the idea. I'd never been a housewife but looked forward to being a loving wife to John and a stepmother to his children. And now I'd have free time to pursue more of the things I enjoyed such as painting.

Since John's medical practice was in Milwaukee, that meant spending a lot of time there. So I made the decision to sell Café de France. Sure, it had been a labor of love but also a huge responsibility. If I could find the right buyer, I'd be happy to see the restaurant continue its success.

Once I made the decision to sell the restaurant, I had several buyers who were interested. But the one I eventually settled on was the right choice. Dominique, my waitress, had taken over as the manager and had also brought in her sister-in-law to help. I trusted them. Dominique was both a hard worker and a fine friend. She confided in me, "If I had the money, I'd buy your restaurant!"

I mentioned this to John. He agreed that it made sense to sell to Dominique and her husband, German. We drew up terms to sell to them on credit and financed it ourselves. This made my heart swell with joy. We were helping them with their dream, which I believed in. Dominque and German ran the restaurant for many successful years.

A new chapter unfolded in my life. John bought a home in Waukesha, Wisconsin, about an hour away from the hospital where he worked. It was our first home together and was a very lovely big house, fit for a king and queen. Some of the windows were so high that we had to hire a special crew to clean them once a month.

Life with Beth and Mike was a mixed bag. I got along okay with Mike, who spent a lot of time on his physical recovery after his terrible accident. We sometimes worked out in the same gym, and I helped him push through the workouts. I was sure his physical therapy was difficult but also quite necessary.

Beth, on the other hand, was more challenging. She wanted me out of the way and, as I mentioned, didn't like sharing her father with me. Beth kept a serious face and an angry glare directed at me. I couldn't blame her. She had already lived through the divorce of her parents, which had been difficult for everyone in her family.

Since I wasn't working, I found myself painting more and more, even joining the Jane Studio in Milwaukee where I received practice and instruction. I met Simone Rogina there, a very special student. She was French-born, and with that connection, we got along famously. Sometimes it made other students upset if we spoke French, but we enjoyed the conversations. We both also spoke Spanish fluently, so sometimes, just for fun, we switched between the languages. Simone was a delight and a talented artist. I was always grateful for the time I took to develop my painting skills. It was something I was passionate about and, even after many years, still enjoy.

I wasn't ready to spend cold winters in Wisconsin. John understood that. Besides, he enjoyed time in Florida and in warmer climes. Fortunately, his schedule allowed us to get away frequently.

In 1987, we took a trip to Jamaica, bringing Mike and Beth along with three other friends. That was a good time and helped all of us to bond. John was also an avid outdoors enthusiast, and I recall a deer expedition at his hunting camp, also in 1987.

We were in Miami at a boat show in 1988. John had been searching for the right sailboat. It was a dream of his to sail, not just for the exhilaration but also with a purpose. He was an accomplished sailor and had spent lots of time on the lakes of Wisconsin as well as on the Great Lakes. I was an avid swimmer and loved the ocean, undoubtedly a passion I'd developed as a youngster in Morocco. John, I knew, hoped to someday sail around the world.

As a caring doctor, he wanted to find ways to help those in need, so John began talking with physicians who helped the poor in South America. These people had no access to X-ray equipment, and John had an idea that someday he'd take one with him on a trip.

He finally found the sailboat he wanted—a fifty-footer. He decided a test run would be a good idea, so we booked a private cruise to the Bahamas where he could try the boat out with the help of a captain.

Since we planned to spend as much time as we could in Florida, it made sense to look for a vacation home there, and we found one in Key Largo on Mutiny Place. It had easy access to the ocean, and John liked the idea that he could keep his sailboat docked at our home.

Maybe it was a stroke of luck or fate. Regardless, we were lucky to still be in Milwaukee in September 1989 when a catastrophic event happened that changed our plans for good.

Hurricane Hugo was a powerful category 5 storm that wreaked immense havoc and devastation. The damage was historic and widespread across the northeastern Caribbean and southeastern United States. It caused $11 billion in damage and killed sixty-seven people.

After that hurricane, we gave up on the idea of a Florida home. Instead, we decided to build our retirement house in Arkansas. John had relatives there, including his Aunt Bess, some cousins, and his father, Alva Winters.

48

Moving to Arkansas

John's dad was a very dear man. At one time, in 1995, he was the oldest living former Arkansas Razorback. That was the name of the University of Arkansas's football team, which had a storied history. The razorback was adopted as the team's mascot in 1909 when, after a big win the coach at the time, Hugo Bezdek, stated that they played like a wild band of razorback hogs. Alva Winters played for them in the 1920s and in 1928 was the captain of the team, so he must have been good.

John resembled his father, just younger. They were both handsome men and had similar personalities. One of the reasons we decided to move to Arkansas was to be closer to this man and other relatives. John's father was born in Traskwood, Arkansas, and had worked as an electrical engineer. No doubt John had learned to fix things from his dad.

At the time, his father was still healthy and active, but because he was elderly, we recognized that taking care of him would someday become a priority. He'd been a good model for this, since he'd been the caregiver for his wife. Alva was one of the sweetest and kindest men I'd ever known.

Relocating to Arkansas also gave John a chance to be close to his Aunt Bess. In her early nineties then, Bess Wolf was fun to be around, was the sister of John's mother, and was a real Southern beauty. Her musical talent was impressive, and she entertained us by playing on glasses and the piano. The music from her running her fingers around the rims of glasses with different amounts of water made a particularly ethereal sound.

Aunt Bess had been married to John Quincy Wolf and had two daughters who lived in Memphis. Later, Adele, the eldest, moved to be closer to her mother. Aunt Bess had a fine country home on the White River in Batesville.

I tried hard to like Adele, but right from the start she was aggressive anytime I was around her mom, which made me feel uncomfortable. For some reason, she didn't want me to be close to Bess.

It was during a summer vacation, when Adele and Bess visited us in Milwaukee, that Adele made a big mistake. We were having a great time in Waukesha, but the day Adele was leaving, she went into the basement of our house with John. I'd stored several of my old paintings in a corner, didn't think they were good enough to save, and was planning to burn them. Adele, however, started loading them into her van without asking. I tried to tell her they weren't good enough, just trash, but she took them, anyway! That rubbed me the wrong way. I never got along with her after that and didn't enjoy being around her. She lacked the grace and kindness of her mother.

In 1993, John took a part-time job in the radiology department in Batesville's hospital. Aunt Bess introduced John to the hospital director. They were thrilled to have him, since he was a very experienced radiologist and had practiced nuclear medicine for many years at West Allis. It gave them more expertise as well as someone who could cover vacations for their other two doctors. John loved the idea of being a country doctor. The flexibility of part-time work gave him the time he needed to help build our home as well as finance our dreams.

That year we purchased eighty-three acres in Arkansas. It was a beautiful area in Desha that I fell in love with right away. There was lots of room for animals and a place to enjoy nature, both quite important to John and me. His father was happy, too. He and John made plans to build a mausoleum on the farm. Then they could move the remains of John's mother there. And it would be a good future eternal resting place for all of us.

Arkansas was a wonderful place to retire. The cost of living was reasonable, and the state had many scenic areas. We got all four seasons, but winters were mild compared to Milwaukee's. By now, it should be apparent how important that was to me.

John had fond memories of spending summers with his family in Batesville. The pace of living was perfect. Country folks were typically friendly with good old-fashioned manners. They liked life in slow motion and also loved music.

Our county was dry, but there were local bootleggers. We never felt lonely driving around. People saluted us as we passed by. It was as if no one was a stranger.

We had to make several trips to move our household from Wisconsin to Arkansas. Our home sold immediately, which was good. Everything was coming together. John had his new job. We also brought his dad to live nearby. Taking care of Grandpa Winters, as I liked to call him, was a priority. He'd been living in Little Rock, the state capital, but moved to our farm while we were between the two places. We bought a mobile home to live in temporarily until we could build our future home on the farm.

Planning our retirement was fun. It was like that with everything I did with John. He wanted me to be happy and laid out the red carpet. I know I made some people upset. At the time, I wondered why, but I came to understand I was living a fairy tale and enjoyed being spoiled.

John was proud of me and I of him. We never competed with each other. He amazed me with all he was able to do. John had many talents, not just as a doctor but also doing things like building a shed or repairing electronic machinery. He had a kind voice and a lovely heart, and being around him gave me peace and joy.

I didn't know people could be so good. My life had been tumultuous, and there were many people who had hurt me or that I couldn't trust. I was on guard all the time. There had been a few kind souls over the years, and I was grateful for them. However, dealing with bullies and mean people had made me a fighter.

There hadn't been much formal education in my life. I never finished high school. However, I was always an avid reader of books, newspapers, and whatever sparked my interest. The world was my school.

John didn't care that I didn't have much formal schooling. He loved my cooking and our time together picking a good bottle of wine. He was good at that and quickly learned that a cold bottle of champagne was often my first choice and a favorite.

We loved meeting new people and made a few fantastic friends. Life was going so well. We'd been married for eight years, and to me, all that time was bliss. Every day was like a visit to Disneyland!

John was the one true love I'd been searching for. We never had an argument. Maybe that sounded unrealistic, but it was true. Each day was blessed. He was another miracle in my life.

49

Bad News

Life was moving along well in our transition from Wisconsin to Arkansas. John and I were both looking forward to settling into our new life on the farm. However, we still had to split time between the two places. John had obligations to complete with the hospital in Milwaukee. He was a man of his word, another thing I admired about him.

Although we'd purchased the property in Arkansas in 1993, it took most of 1994 and even into 1995 to finish things up. While we were in Wisconsin, one of my painting friends had lunch with us. John was home but couldn't stay. He had to leave for work. It was his last week at West Allis Hospital in Milwaukee after more than twenty years. As soon as he departed, my friend asked, "Is John okay? He looks so pale."

"Gosh, you're right. He doesn't look well! But we just returned from Arkansas and John drove all the whole way, never complaining. He's probably just tired."

It was a reasonable explanation, but I suddenly felt cold and scared. In a matter of seconds, it was as if I already knew something terrible was going to crush me. I hated the premonition, but I just knew it! After my friend left, I had to call my beloved husband on his car phone. When he picked up, I said, "John, while you're at work, please get a medical checkup."

"Why?"

"Just do it, please."

He sighed. "I'm just tired, what with our moving and all, but I'm okay."

That was what I'd told my friend, and it was sensible. Our many trips between Wisconsin and Arkansas would have been hard and stressful for anyone. John had never really been sick in his life. He thought he was untouchable. I wanted so hard to believe that. However, I couldn't let it go. "Please get a checkup and make sure they test your blood!"

"I will if it'll make you happy."

I busied myself the rest of the day packing boxes with three movers. But I stayed near the phone, hoping John would call before returning home.

The phone remained silent.

Finally, around nine or ten that night, I heard the garage door open and his car pull inside. I was in the kitchen preparing our dinner when he opened the door. He greeted me with a grim expression. "Sit down, please."

Again that cold and scary feeling came over me.

"It's not good news. I am sick. I have no platelets. I'm dying."

John wasn't being dramatic. After all, he was an experienced radiologist. He knew what test results meant. It was leukemia, and the prognosis wasn't good. The pain of that moment hit me hard. I was pretty sure I lost it but couldn't remember the details. Probably I was blocking it out.

I did recall John talking to Terry Power, my daughter Murielle's husband. Ever mindful of the welfare of others, he was already making plans.

When John got sick, we'd been married for eight years. As I mentioned earlier, it seemed that my life moved in cycles of eight years. And suddenly, it felt as if everything was collapsing. It was the worst timing. Our home was sold, and the movers were scheduled the following Monday to load our furniture and deliver it to Desha.

John was still on call. When the phone rang, he appeared concerned. "What's wrong?" I asked.

"I have to go. A seventeen-year-old shot himself in the head."

"Let me go with you. We can take the van and our dogs to keep you company." It was a forty-five-minute drive to the hospital, and I was worried about him.

We all jumped in the van and drove to West Allis. On the way, I put a CD in and turned up the music. It was a Christmas song, and we both sang to Jesus as if it were Christmastime in the middle of the year.

"Why me, John? Why did you pick me? There are so many young and beautiful nurses."

"I don't love any of them. I love you!"

That was enough for me.

50

The Voice

The next months were hard, no doubt about it. During that time in our Wisconsin home, something strange began to happen. I started waking up every night at exactly the same time—3:00 a.m. At first I didn't know what was going on. Why that time?

On those nights, John slept while I quietly walked downstairs to the studio we'd attached to the house. It was originally an in-law quarters, but we'd turned it into my studio, a quiet place where I could paint and be creative.

I spent the time playing with paint and talking to the TV. And I kept hearing a voice. Of course, it was in my head, but it was telling me, "John's going to die. I'm taking your husband away from you."

This happened for days. Every night at 3:00 a.m., I awakened and *heard* the same message. I couldn't explain it, but it was real to me. I'd stay in my studio for a couple of hours, just painting, and finally, the voice disappeared. Was I losing my mind? Should I see a shrink?

Although the voice was frightening, it also had a reassuring quality, as if I were speaking to a friend. Sadly, what the voice was telling me was true.

John spent three months of 1995 at West Allis Hospital getting aggressive treatment for leukemia. He'd worked there for more than two decades and was now a patient fighting for his life. John underwent chemotherapy, lost all his beautiful hair, and got progressively weaker.

I booked a hotel near the hospital where I could take showers and steal a couple of hours of sleep. But I found it hard to stay away from John and spent much of that time sleeping on a couch next to him.

After three months, we were told the leukemia was in remission. So we decided it was time to finally go to our new place in Arkansas. It would be awesome to see John there. We intended to stay in the mobile home we'd bought for our temporary quarters before building a house.

When we arrived at our property, a golf cart was waiting for us. John loved using it to drive around our land. Right away, he wanted to get moving on various plans he had such as building a chapel and family mausoleum. He even made an appointment with a builder to discuss all of that.

One day, as we were walking around the farm, John suddenly stopped to view what was before him.

"What would you want in this location?" I asked him.

"A cemetery. This would be a good spot for it."

"And a chapel!" I chimed in.

"Great idea!"

Over the next month, John got stronger. We discussed doing some of the things we'd always wanted to do and put together a bucket list.

We took a sailing trip to the Bahamas—John, me, and a captain hired by the boat owner. However, it ended up being something of a nightmare, with the three of us in the middle of a violent storm, the captain drunk!

A trip overseas for a cruise was also proposed. It would be special with various stops: Rome, Naples, Sicily, Malta, and Athens. It had always been a dream of John's to sail the Mediterranean.

Before we committed to the cruise, I contacted John's doctor for advice to make sure it was okay. "Go ahead!" the doctor told me. "Enjoy the time you have left." That was reassuring.

One of our trip's special events was a visit to the Vatican in Rome where we met with Pope John Paul II in his private residence at Castel Gandolfo.

The cruise was fantastic! John really enjoyed it, and thankfully, he was doing well. He even took the time to talk about our future. John was realistic, but that didn't stop him from discussing plans.

We both wondered what was going to happen, but who could predict the future? John had acute myeloid leukemia 7, the worst kind. It was almost always a killer, but he had the right attitude. He knew the end was a matter of months, maybe even weeks, but decided to live each day fully. As for me, I was a bit lost and unsure what to do, yet it felt as if every moment with John gave me strength to deal with the situation. It provided me with the faith to handle each moment. By the time the cruise was over, I was stronger and was meditating daily, which helped me find peace.

The cruise finished in Athens from where we flew to Paris. In Athens, we made a connection to the south of France to my sister's home in the village of Parnac. Mom, France, and other family members were waiting for us.

We partied and enjoyed the best food and French wine. Once again, I was reminded that we should make the most of every day, which really hit home the next morning.

John woke up feeling very sick! As a doctor, he knew immediately he had to find a lab to have his blood tested. Sure enough, the results revealed that he had no platelets. We were in trouble, and the only thing to do was get him to a hospital for treatment.

I arranged for a flight to Paris where John could get a bed at the American Hospital. My brothers, Alain and Richard, would be waiting for us at the airport. My mother and sister cried as they said goodbye to John and me. Our flight was the next day.

John was grateful that he could speak English to the caretakers at the American Hospital. This private, not-for-profit community hospital had been founded in 1906 and was located in Neuilly-sur-Seine in the western suburbs of Paris. It was certified under the French healthcare system.

During this time in 1995, there was a lot of tension between some Muslim factions and France and the United States. There had been bomb scares at the airport, so my brothers drove me back to our mother's place to spend the night.

The next morning, I arrived at the hospital at seven. John had received a blood transfusion and platelets, and we could tell he was feeling better. He was very glad to see us.

The nurses were very helpful. Before my brothers wheeled John to the taxi, one of them came over, hugged me, and pressed something into my hand. "These are morphine pills for the trip. You'll need them." What an angel.

When we arrived at Charles de Gaulle Airport, my brothers said their goodbyes. John was weak and stayed in a wheelchair, so we immediately boarded our plane. I could tell he was in pain, but he never complained and held my hand tightly. It was a difficult trip, and several times he asked for one of the morphine pills. It made me so grateful to the nurse, and in my heart, I knew I'd never stop thanking him. He'd taken a chance giving me the morphine, but it really helped John to endure the lengthy trip.

As soon as our flight touched down, we arranged to go to a hospital in Memphis where John could receive more platelets.

51

Preparing to Say Goodbye

It became clear that we needed to prepare to say goodbye to John. I reserved four rooms at a hotel near the Memphis hospital. Soon, family began arriving. Mom flew in first, followed by Alva Winters, my father-in-law. He was always so loving and supportive and had already dealt with the passing of his beloved wife of many years. Also arriving were Murielle and John's son, Mike. Unfortunately, his daughter, Beth, and Aunt Bess weren't able to travel to Memphis. Neither could Bruno Junior. But it was good that Bob and Beverly, John's two very good friends, the ones who had introduced us years before at Café de France, were able to be there.

It was good to have them all there. Everyone tried to help, but I didn't want to accept that John was dying. Eventually, Murielle asked me to tell John it was time to let go. She, my mom, and Beverly all believed John was holding on, waiting for me to say my final goodbye.

I couldn't understand that at the time. I'd never heard such nonsense and refused to listen to them. I wished they'd stop talking about it. I was clearly in denial of the end.

Once, when I was at John's bedside, he said, summoning up all his strength, "I love you!"

Finally, I realized I had to say a last goodbye. I put my arm around his neck and held him as he passed.

John, the love of my life, died at noon on a Sunday in 1995 in Memphis, Tennessee. We'd been married for a very good eight years, but it was all too short! I felt as if I died that day, as well.

In those few years we had together, we never had an argument. Each day was a blessing. Every day was like a visit to Disneyland! He was yet another miracle in my life, the love I'd always been searching for.

52

After John and Life on the Farm

Sadly, John didn't live long enough for us to build our house on the farm in Desha. I felt it important to continue living there. It was to be our place of retirement where we could spend our golden years together.

Among the good things John left me were two Rottweilers, my loving dogs, Alex and Java. They were a big factor in my ability to continue by myself in the hills of Arkansas after John's death and later that of his father. Alex was wide and stocky and looked like a lion. He was my protector. Java was a bit smaller but could be just as intimidating. I also had nature and the good pace of country living to help me in those years after John's passing.

In many ways, I stayed quite busy and had some interesting experiences with real business success. I raised some livestock and had many wonderful animals, especially sheep, though I no longer keep a large group of them, just a few now. I enjoy the lively and lovely lambs.

My entrepreneurial spirit came alive, and I became sort of a local celebrity, the Frenchwoman with cooking skills and the ability to produce amazing pesto and other herb oils. That could be another book!

A chapel was built along with a cemetery for our beloved family members who had died. There, in the splendor of nature, I can truly feel God's presence while also remembering the loved ones who have passed on.

Eventually, I also became a strong family presence for grandchildren and great-grandchildren. There were some heartbreaking things that happened along the way. That, I've learned, is the nature of life. There are ups and downs, all of which have helped to further my spiritual growth.

One of the things for which I feel quite blessed was the time I had with John's father. Alva Winters was also grieving, both for his wife and for his only son. He had a broken heart just like me.

I decided to do all I could for him. He also did a lot for me with his amazing kindness. We spent many afternoons together as he drove us around the farm in an electric golf cart. I did my part by cooking the best food just for him. And I kept him talking about his life and family. He was very sweet and kind. I just loved the old man!

One day, I asked him, "Grandpa, why are you so nice to me?"

"Because you made my son happy!"

That was the best compliment anyone had ever given me.

My father-in-law was pure love for family, and I saw that John had had the best example.

53

Life Lessons Learned

I've learned many lessons in my life. One of prime importance is that we're all here to do the best we can. Everyone has choices. We all sometimes make mistakes. But it's all part of the journey, the great tapestry of life.

Now, in my later years, I do my best to live in peace and harmony. Yes, I'm human and sometimes get stressed. I hope I'm better at responding well. I think so and have John and others who have been important to me to thank for helping me discover the ways to respond instead of react.

I've also learned it's important to stand up for yourself and for what's right. Everyone deserves respect. We have to forgive when we're hurt and be willing to make amends when we've wronged others.

My life has been full. There have been many extraordinary moments and experiences that have shaped who I am today. I draw strength from those times, both the good and the bad. It's all part of life.

For my family and friends, I leave this tale of my life so that they can better know who I am and what my life has been about. Perhaps they'll draw some life lessons of their own from what I've shared.

I thank all those who read my story and am grateful for the opportunity to share it. Now, readers, go and live your lives fully, for it's the gift we each receive at birth.

ACKNOWLEDGMENTS

To my family and friends I thank you for your love and encouragement. Your belief in me has been a constant source of strength and inspiration.

I also am grateful for my co-writer, T. M. Gilbert. Your interest in my life story motivated me to share my ideas with the world.

Lastly, thank you to all my readers and supporters. I hope you find something in my memoir that touches your heart and helps you on with your journey.

www.ingramcontent.com/pod-product-compliance
Lightning Source LLC
Chambersburg PA
CBHW050326010526
44119CB00030B/426/J